THE REMNANT

CLIFFORD GOLDSTEIN

Biblical reality
or wishful thinking?

Pacific Press Publishing Association
Boise, Idaho
Oshawa, Ontario, Canada

Edited by B. Russell Holt
Designed by Tim Larson
Cover art by Tim Larson
Typeset in 10/12 Janson

Library of Congress Cataloging-in-Publication Data:
Goldstein, Clifford.
    The Remnant : biblical reality or wishful thinking? / Clifford
Goldstein.
            p.   cm.
      ISBN 0-8163-1192-7
      1. Seventh-day Adventists—Doctrines. 2. Adventists—Doc-
trines. 3. Sabbatarians—Doctrines. 4. Remnant (Theology)
I. Title.
BX6154.G635   1994
286.7'32—dc20
                                                          93-23217
                                                            CIP

94 95 96 97 98 • 5 4 3 2 1

For those who might find healing
in these words . . .

Contents

Murder in the Remnant Church

1

• A twelve-year-old is repeatedly dragged into bed by her remnant-church father while her remnant-church mom does nothing.

• A young woman who has read remnant-church literature comes to Sabbath worship. No one greets her, asks her name, or talks to her—except an elderly saint who sneers at the pearls dangling from her neck.

• A child cries. His parents, both leaders in the local remnant church, divorce after years of smiling in public and fighting at home.

• A young adult burns with hatred toward the remnant. Her father—head elder, Sabbath School teacher, and Pathfinder leader—beats his wife and then goes out and gives Bible studies.

• A remnant-church minister—*minister!*—is arrested for robbing a bank.

• A teacher at a remnant-church academy is caught in bed with another man's wife. The enraged husband strangles him.

• Some, denouncing the doctrines of the remnant, accuse it of heresy; others, claiming that it has deviated doctrinally, accuse it of apostasy.

• A remnant-church member opens his motorcycle dealership on Sabbath.

• Parents torture themselves with remorse; after years of sacrificing to send their children to remnant schools, they see all of them renounce the remnant faith.

• Standing before a remnant-church hospital that performs abortions, a Christian holds a sign that says, "Thou shalt not kill."

• A remnant-church youth pastor faces charges of sexual relations with an adolescent girl.

• *Vanity Fair* runs an article about a southern California doctor arrested for murdering a patient in his office. The magazine states that the doctor had been a pillar in his community and in "the Seventh-day Adventist Church"—the remnant church.

These sordid clips barely begin to catalog the litany of lies uttered and sins committed by God's "great Advent family," those preparing for translation at Christ's second coming. How many members could write a chapter, if not a book, about what has been done by those who cloak themselves, not only under the mantle of Christianity but under the folds of the "remnant church"? No doubt, Adventist young people could write some of the bitterest, most painful volumes.

As a result, many have been asking, "How can all these sins—incest, adultery, even murder—be in the remnant church?"

Or—is it *really* the remnant church?

2

From their beginning as a scattered, fledgling group of leftover Millerites, Seventh-day Adventists have referred to themselves as the *remnant*. Even before formally instituting a church, the pioneers called themselves the remnant. Perhaps the earliest use of the term was in an 1846 pamphlet titled "To the Little Remnant Scattered Abroad." In 1849, Joseph Bates used Revelation 12:17, which points to those who "keep the commandments of God, and have the testimony of Jesus" in describing Adventists as "the remnant."[1]

In 1853, Ellen White referred to Sabbath-keeping Adventists as "the remnant people of God."[2] In 1855, when J. M. Stephenson left the movement, he was urged to reconsider severing himself from "the remnant people of God."[3] In 1857, James White wrote that the Laodicean message was "a special call to the remnant," and he urged Adventists to obey its counsel.[4] In 1860, when pondering a name for their new church, the pioneers considered "the Remnant."[5] Adventists adopted the remnant motif, according to historian P. Gerard Damsteegt, because it "indicated the uniqueness of Sabbatarian Adventists as the remnant of God's people who continued to adhere to the major positions of the Advent movement."[6]

Through the years, the word *remnant*, or the phrase *the remnant church*, has become the definitive, self-proclaimed mark of Seventh-day Adventists. For a century and a half, books and periodicals rolling off our presses have called this movement "the remnant church." On the baptismal certificate, first issued in the early 1940s, the thirteenth question of the Baptismal Vow asked, "Do you believe that the Seventh-day Adventist Church constitutes the remnant church, and do

11

you desire to be accepted into its membership?" Today the certificate asks if the baptismal candidate believes that the Seventh-day Adventist Church is the "remnant church of Bible prophecy?"

The denomination officially established the concept of the remnant as doctrine when the 1980 General Conference session in Dallas proclaimed Adventism to be the "remnant [that] has been called out to keep the commandments of God and the faith of Jesus." This wording became the twelfth of the twenty-seven fundamental beliefs:

> The universal church is composed of all who truly believe in Christ, but in the last days, a time of widespread apostasy, a remnant has been called out to keep the commandments of God and the faith of Jesus. This remnant announces the arrival of the judgment hour, proclaims salvation through Christ, and heralds the approach of His second advent. This proclamation is symbolized by the three angels of Revelation 14; it coincides with the work of judgment in heaven and results in a work of repentance and reform on earth. Every believer is called to have a personal part in this worldwide witness.[7]

Adventists claim the title "the remnant" or "the remnant church" *exclusively* as their own. The church does not believe any other corporate body or church is the remnant, though Adventists concede "we do not believe that we alone constitute the true children of God—that we are the only true Christians—on earth today."[8] The Adventist church does teach, however, that all other denominations are in some degree of theological apostasy, that Adventism alone possesses "the present truth," and that "through the remnant church He [God] proclaims a message that is to restore His true worship by calling His people out of the apostasy and preparing them for Christ's return."[9]

Of course, Seventh-day Adventists are not the only ones making exclusive declarations about themselves. The Mormons proclaim that they are the true, restored church (with a prophet and health message, to boot), alone proclaiming the "everlasting gospel" of Revelation 14 in its pure, primitive form. Jehovah's Witnesses teach that only they have the truth and that all other denominations are Babylon. The Catholic church believes that it is the original, mother church and that Protestants have deviated from the faith once delivered to the saints.

Obviously, a body declaring something about itself doesn't make it so. "A group is not a remnant," writes Bruce Moyer, "simply because it calls itself a 'remnant.' It is a remnant only when it behaves as a remnant, prophetic people should behave."[10]

In recent years, some within the church have questioned the Adventist identification of itself as the remnant. An article in the *Adventist Review* says, "God is looking for a remnant today. We can be that remnant,"[11] implying that the church, as it stands now, isn't. Many, seeing worldliness, theological compromise, and lack of commitment to our present-truth message are tempted to doubt the church's remnant status. Others argue that the phrase is triumphalistic, exclusive, and fosters spiritual pride and arrogance. Others, especially the young, see sin, hypocrisy, legalism, coldness, lack of love, and dissension in the church; they ask, understandably, *How can this be the remnant church?*

Also, we Adventists claim that we are "the remnant church of Bible prophecy," yet we also call ourselves the Laodicean church. Are we both? "Laodicea" certainly seems to fit reality better than does "the remnant church." Laodicea—the church which says "I am rich, have become wealthy, and have need of nothing" yet is really "wretched, miserable, poor, blind, and naked" (Revelation 3:17, NKJV)—is an apt description of Adventism. Had those incidents listed at the beginning of this chapter substituted "Laodicean church" for "remnant church," they would have read:

• A young woman who has read Laodicean-church literature comes to Sabbath worship. No one greets her, asks her name, or talks to her—except an elderly saint who sneers at the pearls dangling from her neck.

• A child cries. His parents, both leaders in the local Laodicean church, divorce after years of smiling in public and fighting at home.

Somehow, these sentences make better sense than the first versions do.

The Seventh-day Adventist self-identification as Laodicea seems to contradict its perception of itself as the remnant. The Lord threatens to "spew out" Laodicea (Revelation 3:16), while promising that the remnant, those who get the "victory over the beast, and over his image and over his mark and over the number of his name," will stand upon the sea of glass, "having the harps of God" (Revelation 15:2).

How can we be both? Or can we?

This book examines the remnant. It traces the biblical concept of the remnant from the beginning to the end of time, in an attempt to answer these questions: Who is the remnant? What factors determine the remnant? Do you have to be holy to be part of the remnant? Can the remnant include the unconverted as well as the converted? Does the idea of a "remnant within a remnant" have any validity? Can the remnant apostatize? Is Laodicea the remnant?

Is *Seventh-day Adventism* the remnant? Or do we need, in light of our present condition, to reexamine the claim?

---

1. Joseph Bates, *A Seal of the Living God* (New Bedford, Mass., 1849), 45-56.

2. *Spiritual Gifts*, 2:168, 169.

3. *The Review and Herald*, 18 December 1855, 93.

4. Ibid., 8 January 1857, 75.

5. Ibid., 25 September 1860, 148.

6. P. Gerard Damsteegt, *Foundations of the Seventh-day Adventist Movement* (Grand Rapids: Eerdmans, 1977), 243.

7. *Seventh-day Adventists Believe: A Biblical Exposition of 27 Fundamental Doctrines* (Washington, D.C.: General Conference of SDAs, 1988), 152.

8. *Questions on Doctrine* (Washington, D.C.: Review and Herald Publishing Association, 1957), 187.

9. *Seventh-day Adventists Believe*, 168.

10. Bruce Moyer, "Love in Practice," *Adventist Review*, 29 March 1990, 11.

11. Ibid., 12.

The Remnant Among the Nations

3

"T"he remnant theme," writes Gerhard Hasel, "moves through the Bible from Genesis to Revelation as a red thread."[1] Six different Hebrew roots form dozens of words[2] used hundreds of times in all sorts of contexts in the Old Testament (though the remnant *theme* itself can be traced even without the use of any of these words). It is a rich, complicated topic that has been debated among scholars for years.

Noah's family formed the first remnant noted in Scripture. After "every living substance" (Genesis 7:4) was blotted out, only Noah and his clan survived: "And *was left*[3] only Noah and those with him in the ark" (Genesis 7:23), which included his wife, sons, and daughters-in-law.[4]

Why only these?

First, Scripture says that Noah was a "just man and perfect in his generations, and [that] Noah walked with God" (Genesis 6:9). Second, the Lord said to Noah "thee have I seen righteous before me in this generation" (Genesis 7:1). And, finally, Noah did "all that God commanded him" (Genesis 6:22).

No wonder, then, that the Lord said to Noah, "With thee will I establish my covenant" (Genesis 6:18). A covenant works only if the parties agree to the terms. Though the rest of mankind had "corrupted his way upon the earth" (Genesis 6:12), Noah, who walked with God and did all that God commanded him, agreed to follow his end of the bargain, which included building the boat and then getting into it. Of the untold multitudes on earth, only eight—even after 120 years of warning—entered the ark, which shows that the seven others,

17

besides Noah, were abiding under the covenant as well.

Noah and his family, unlike the rest of the world, believed "present truth," which then consisted of the message that the world was going to be wiped out in a flood. This distinct message, and their adherence to it, helped form their identification as the remnant.

Yet the story doesn't end here. Noah "planted a vineyard: And he drank of the wine and was drunken: and he was uncovered within his tent" (Genesis 9:20, 21). The patriarch wasn't merely nipping at a little red wine with his newly acquired meat diet; he got soused, to the point that he fell asleep and was "uncovered" in his tent. No doubt the Lord forgave Noah's indiscretion, but the incident shows that even Noah, the victorious leader of the remnant, could fall.

Noah's binge, however, was only the beginning. In Ham, who saw "the nakedness of his father" (Genesis 9:22), "filial reverence had long before been cast from his soul, and it [his act] revealed the impiety and vileness of his character."[5] Thus, the original remnant was corrupt from the start, and Noah himself predicted that Ham's offspring would be cursed (see Genesis 9:25-27). Even though Noah had positive things to say about his other two sons and their posterity, their offspring apostatized as well.

Obviously, being part of the remnant did not come about by inheritance or by marriage. Being of remnant blood doesn't make one a member of the remnant family. However righteous Noah was, he couldn't automatically pass his righteousness on to his posterity. His wife, three sons, and daughters-in-law, whatever their intrinsic faults, had to get on the boat of their own choosing. Thus, they too were part of the remnant, in this case consisting only of a small family.

Membership in this "family" remnant, then, came by individual choice. The remnant had to agree to the Lord's terms and then follow them by faith. After the Flood, most of Noah's descendants didn't choose to do so. In rebellion, they began to construct the tower of Babel. Though the Lord had promised that "neither shall all flesh be cut off any more by the waters of a flood" (Genesis 9:11) and painted a rainbow across the sky as a symbol of that promise, they built the tower to secure their own safety in case of another deluge. They didn't believe God's promises or His rainbows. No covenant relationship existed between them and the Lord, as had been the case with Noah's family through whom the first remnant was formed.

1. Gerhard Hasel, "The Remnant in Scripture and the End," *Adventist Affirm*, Fall 1988, 5.

2. Those roots are *sha'ar* ("to remain," "to be left over"), *palat* ("to escape"), *malat* ("slip"), *yathar* ("to remain," "to be left over"), *sarad* ("to escape"), and `*achar* ("to delay," "to tarry"). From these numerous words, such nouns or abstract nouns as "remained," "residue," "escape," "fugitive," "excess," "rest," "hinder," "part" are formed.

3. The root *sha'ar* is the one most commonly used for the remnant, the one that has been studied more intensively than any of the others. In Ezekiel's vision of the slaughter of those in Jerusalem who didn't have the mark upon their foreheads, the prophet fell upon his face and cried, "Ah Lord God! wilt thou destroy all the *residue* (from *sha'ar*) of Israel in thy pouring out of thy fury upon Jerusalem?" (Ezekiel 9:8).

4. Author's translation.

5. *Patriarchs and Prophets*, 117.

4

Despite Noah's positive words spoken about his son, Shem ("Blessed be the Lord God of Shem" [Genesis 9:26]), Shem's posterity apostatized. Thus, Abram (later Abraham), a descendant of Shem, had to leave his idolatrous family. "Now the Lord had said unto Abram, Get thee out of thy country, and from thy kindred, and from thy father's house, unto a land that I will show thee" (Genesis 12:1).

As one of the few remaining followers of the "Lord God of Shem," Abraham began a new remnant, coming as he did at the end of the line, genealogically, of Shem's family tree (see Genesis 11). Like Noah before Him, Abraham entered into a covenant relationship with the Lord. "And when Abram was ninety years old and nine, the Lord appeared to Abram, and said unto him, I am the Almighty God; walk before me, and be thou perfect. And I will make my covenant between me and thee, and will multiply thee exceedingly" (Genesis 17:1, 2).

Abraham also had present truth for his time—that the Lord Jehovah was the Creator and that He alone should be worshiped. By following the true God amid a world praying to and worshiping statues of wood and stone, Abraham enjoyed, by far, the greatest light of his generation.

Despite his faults (lying to Pharaoh, not trusting God's promises and, instead, taking Hagar as his wife), Abraham was someone who maintained a saving relationship with the Lord amid a world that didn't. In this sense, he formed a new line, a family remnant that alone would preserve the worship of Yahweh as long as it remained faithful to the covenant conditions: "For I know him, that he will command his

21

children and his household after him, and they shall keep the way of the Lord, to do justice and judgment; that the Lord may bring upon Abraham that which he hath spoken of him" (Genesis 18:19).

These verses show that the Lord's call to Abraham wasn't arbitrary. "I know him," the Lord said, "that he will command his household after him." The Lord testified to Abraham's character and how it would affect his offspring. Yet the Lord could bring upon Abraham "that which he hath spoken of him" only by his (and his posterity's) obedience. Abraham's faith and standing with God wouldn't automatically be passed on to his seed. Anyone can be born into a remnant family (or church), but one is only "born again" into the remnant faith.

5

Abraham's promised line came out of his son Isaac, whose seed formed that "great and mighty nation" which alone preserved the true faith amid pagan and idolatrous peoples. In contrast, Ishmael's descendants did not worship God (see Genesis 25). "My covenant will I establish with Isaac, which Sarah shall bear unto thee at this set time in the next year," God declared (Genesis 17:21). This was no arbitrary decree, a prophecy of predestination that guaranteed Isaac a covenant relationship with the Lord. Isaac would have to choose to cooperate, so that the Lord could "bring upon Abraham that which he hath spoken of him" (Genesis 18:19). If the covenant was to be established with Isaac, he must obey—and he did. Therefore, the Lord renewed to Isaac the promises He had made to Abraham.

This privilege didn't automatically pass on to Isaac's offspring. Not all of Isaac's children formed the remnant. His first two boys, Esau and Jacob, were fraternal twins. "Two nations are in thy womb" the Lord told Rebekah (Genesis 25:23). One of them fathered a pagan nation; the other, the remnant. What made the difference?

Esau was born first, and to him belonged the birthright, the same special privileges and promises that Abraham passed on to Isaac. As with Noah, Abraham, and Isaac, these promises were covenantal in nature. Yet, for "one morsel of meat he [Esau] sold his birthright" (Hebrews 12:16). He made a conscious choice not to follow the Lord, in spite of the unique opportunities offered him.

Jacob, his brother, highly esteemed the promises. Although he obtained them by fraud (see Genesis 27), his actions showed how much he revered them. Jacob repented, and his life showed his determination to follow the Lord despite the negative consequences that resulted from his deception.

Esau, tired from a day of hunting, cast off the blessings for a moment's gratification; Jacob, in contrast, wrestled all night with the Lord rather than lose them. "I will not let thee go," he said to the Lord, "except thou bless me" (Genesis 32:26). No wonder Esau didn't become the heir of the promises, and Jacob did. No wonder that Esau walked in darkness, and Jacob in light. No wonder that Esau's seed formed a pagan nation (see Genesis 36:8), and Jacob's—the remnant.

6

The remnant theme appears next in Scripture in connection with Joseph. After his brothers had entered Egypt to seek relief from the famine, Joseph—having tested their fidelity, and the depth of their repentance—finally revealed himself. He then said, "God sent me before you, to preserve for you *a remnant* on the earth, and to keep alive for you many survivors" (Genesis 45:7).*

His brothers certainly didn't show the faith of Abraham, Isaac, and Jacob, the remnant that preceded them. Selling Joseph into slavery and then lying to their father about it made Noah, Abraham, and Jacob, even at their worst, seem ready for translation. Yet Scripture refers to Joseph's brothers as a "remnant"?

Yes, because despite the heinousness of their crime, these men had matured, grown in character, and even showed true repentance, as seen in their dealings with Joseph. When Joseph—still concealing his identity—demanded that they bring their younger brother to him, they allowed themselves to be cast into prison, rather than bring additional sorrow on their father by the loss of another son.

Also, they accused themselves bitterly of their sin against Joseph, showing their repentance. "We are verily guilty concerning our brother, in that we saw the anguish of his soul, when he besought us, and we would not hear; therefore is this distress come upon us" (Genesis 42:21).

When finally they did bring Benjamin, Joseph made a meal in which he gave Benjamin, the youngest, more food than the rest of his brothers. "And he took and sent messes unto them from before him: but Benjamin's mess was five times so much as any of their's" (Genesis

43:34). Joseph wanted to see if they manifested the same envy toward Benjamin, the youngest, as they had shown toward him. They didn't, because the next verse says that "they drank, and were merry with him" (verse 35).

Then, when he thought Benjamin was to be kept as a slave, Judah offered himself instead. "Now therefore, I pray thee, let thy servant abide instead of the lad a bondman to my lord; and let the lad go up with his brethren. For how shall I go up to my father, and the lad be not with me? lest peradventure I see the evil that shall come on my father" (Genesis 44:33, 34).

Joseph, now satisfied about the change in his brothers, revealed his identity. Afterward, the whole family came to Egypt, where they survived the famine. This remnant family—walking alone in the present truth that Yahweh was the Creator (while the rest of the world worshiped false gods)—became the nation of Israel.

---

* Author's translation.

7

At Sinai, the children of Israel, newly escaped from Egypt, entered into a covenant with God not unlike the one God had made with Abraham, Isaac, and Jacob. Indeed, the covenant with Israel at Sinai fulfilled the promises God had made with the patriarchs that their seed would become a "great nation." Now, however, the promises extended to an entire nation, unlike patriarchal times, in which the remnant promises existed only among a few generations of a nuclear family.

"Now therefore," the Lord said to the Hebrews at Sinai, "if ye will obey my voice indeed, and keep my covenant, then ye shall be a peculiar treasure unto me above all people: for all the earth is mine: And ye shall be unto me a kingdom of priests, and an holy nation" (Exodus 19:5, 6).

The Bible gives prominence to Israel; its history is at the center of the Old Testament and much of the New. However, the nation itself was always a minor entity in the ancient Near East. "Palestine represents only a tiny portion of Middle Eastern territory," write John Hayes and J. Max Miller, "and the period of ancient Israelite and Judean history represents only a small segment of the long sweep of Middle Eastern history."[1]

First, the Hebrews were late arrivals in the ancient Near East. "Whatever one says of Israel's origins," writes John Bright, "must be said with full awareness that these lie nowhere near the dawn of history."[2] A dozen Egyptian dynasties had risen and fallen before Israel had sprung from Abraham's loins. By the time the Hebrew nation was born, Egypt's Great Pyramid—two million blocks weighing two and a half tons each—was nearly a thousand years old.

Second, Israel was a relatively unpopulated place compared to the empires around it, such as Babylon and Egypt, whose populations were much larger than the Hebrew nation's ever was. And the masses of all the ancient Near Eastern pagan entities together greatly dwarfed that of the Jewish one.

Third, it was small geographically in relation to the great powers of the ancient world. Maps of the ancient Near East show that, even when the twelve tribes had expanded their borders to their greatest extent, Israel never possessed large amounts of land. Assyria, Babylon, Persia, even Egypt, at their heights, had empires much more vast than the Jews ever did.

Fourth, except for one century when, under the united monarchy of David and Solomon, Israel was a regional force to be reckoned with, it was never a great military power. At best, it was only a local force, able to subdue the small nations around it and, for a while, to keep Egypt in check. At various times in its history, especially after the nation separated into two hostile kingdoms, it was invaded, pillaged, and plundered by Egyptians, Assyrians, Syrians, Babylonians, Persians, Greeks, and finally the Romans.

Thus, Israel's importance lay not in its size, population, or military prowess. What made Israel the center of the Bible was its religion. Israel alone adhered, however fitfully, to the original faith that went back to Abraham, Noah, and Adam. Corporately, it remained the only outpost of a knowledge of God during a time when the true religion of mankind was smothered in an explosion of paganism and idolatry that covered the world with the debris of superstitions and false teaching. In this sense, Israel was "a remnant of the nations,"[3] a leftover amid a world that neither knew the true God nor His doctrine, nor had a relationship with Him.

---

1. John Hayes and J. Max Miller, *A History of Ancient Israel and Judah* (Philadelphia: Westminster, 1986), 25.

2. John Bright, *The History of Israel* (Philadelphia: Westminster Press, 1981), 23.

3. Edgar Johnson, *Aspects of the Remnant Concept in Matthew* (Ph.D. diss., Andrews University, 1984), 27.

8

Israel's role as "a remnant among the nations" best stands out when its faith is contrasted with the paganism surrounding it.

From the Nile to the Euphrates, the ancient Near Easterner worshiped a highly developed pantheon of gods and goddesses that manifested themselves in nature. In a storm was the storm god; in sunshine was the sun god. Just as nature was not peaceful, neither were the gods, who were often given the attributes of men—vengeance, jealousy, inconsistency, passion, and violence. Indeed, these gods were often depicted as killing, fighting, even raping each other.

Then, amid this parade of polytheism, a small nation of ex-slaves, refugees without their own land, wanderers without a country, proclaimed one of the most radical ideas in antiquity: *Shema Yisrael, Adonai Elohanu, Adonai Echad,*" which means, "Hear O Israel, the Lord is God, the Lord is one" (Deuteronomy 6:4).[1]

As radical as this idea was, however, it wasn't new! Monotheism and the worship of Yahweh alone had been the original religion of mankind, the faith of Adam, Eve, Abel, Methuselah, Enoch, and Noah. The Jews—instead of acknowledging a pantheon of gods and goddesses (no word for *goddess* even exists in Hebrew)—worshiped only one God, the Creator, because He *is* the Creator and the only God, the One worshiped from the beginning. This truth had been all but lost amid the polytheism that permeated the ancient Near East. The Hebrews, a remnant nation that clung to the original faith, were the only ones following it. Thus, by worshiping one God only, Yahweh, the Hebrews were not coming up with something new and innovative; they were adhering to something old and original. Polytheism was new.

It was the same with the Jews' rejection of the god-as-nature foolishness. Unlike the pagans, the Hebrew nation didn't identify God as a part of His creation. Instead, they viewed creation as a product of God, not as the carrier or possessor of the qualities of God Himself. As Adam and Eve had done, they learned about Him as Creator and worshiped Him as such.

This concept, too, as different as it was from the nations around them, simply recaptured the original truths that God first gave to mankind in Eden.

Besides their polytheism, the pagans of the ancient Near East were steeped in idolatry. Israel's neighbors had carved armies of idols, gods of wood and stone, to represent the deities whom they served. The ancient Near Easterner might not have seen the idol as the god itself, but only as a representation of that deity in which its spirit would reside, enabling the god to be in different places simultaneously. As a result, the pagan would bow down, offer sacrifices, and pray to statues of bulls, goats, frogs, and even humans. Idolatry was more widespread in the ancient Near Eastern world than Islam is in the modern one.

Yet, while dirt from Egypt was still under their nails, God told the Jews: "You shall not make for yourself any carved image, or any likeness of anything that is in heaven above, or that is in the earth beneath, or that is in the water under the earth; you shall not bow down to them nor serve them" (Exodus 20:4, 5, NKJV).

Isaiah mocked idolaters:

> He hews down cedars for himself, and takes the cypress and the oak. . . . He burns half of it in the fire; with this half he himself and says, "Ah! I am warm, I have seen the fire." And the rest of it he makes into a god, his carved image. He falls down before it and worships it, prays to it and says, "Deliver me, for you are my god" (Isaiah 44:14-17, NKJV).

Here, too, no matter how greatly Israel's faith differed from the nations around them, it wasn't anything new. The Lord never intended for mankind to worship nature. Idolatry represented a later apostasy from the living God.

> Professing themselves to be wise, they became fools, And

changed the glory of the uncorruptible God into an image made like to corruptible man, and to birds, and fourfooted beasts, and creeping things . . . Who changed the truth of God into a lie, and worshipped and served the creature more than the Creator (Romans 1:22, 23, 25).

By rejecting idolatry, Israel was simply restoring the worship of the true God as it had been before it was changed into a "lie," as Paul wrote. The Lord told Adam that he was to "have dominion over the fish of the sea, and over the fowl of the air, and over every living thing that moveth upon the earth" (Genesis 1:28)—not to bow down and worship them. It was only after the fall, when men turned away from the living God, that idolatry surfaced. Thus, far from adhering to a new, radical concept, the Hebrews were merely reaching back to the original faith, before man "changed the glory of the uncorruptible God" into idols.

The ancient Near East was also saturated with magic, divination, and astrology, all used for religious, political, and military purposes. Pagan priests would even study the livers of sheep and other animals to discern the future. If this method became too expensive, other means, such as the configuration of rising smoke from a censer, observations of deformed babies, the shape of water poured on oil, even shooting arrows were forms of magic and divination used to forecast the future.

Again, Israel had radically broken away from the prevailing norm, at least in theory. From the earliest days at Sinai, even before entering the Promised Land, the Jews had been warned against dabbling in the divination and magic so prevalent in the nations around them.

When you come into the land which the Lord your God is giving you, you shall not learn to follow the abominations of those nations. There shall not be found among you anyone who makes his son or his daughter pass through the fire, or one who practices witchcraft, or a soothsayer, or one who interprets omens, or a sorcerer, or one who conjures spells, or a medium, or a spiritist, or one who calls up the dead. . . . For these nations which you will dispossess listened to soothsayers and diviners; but as for you, the Lord your God has not appointed such for you (Deuteronomy 18:9-14, NKJV).

Why?

Because these were not the methods that the Lord had originally chosen to use to communicate with His people. Adam and Eve didn't look at the liver of a lamb to learn about the coming Redeemer. Noah didn't read the stars in order to know how to build the ark. Abraham didn't bring Isaac to Mount Moriah because the shape of oil poured on water told him to. And it wasn't by observing deformed infants that Jacob knew that his seed would inherit Canaan. From the beginning, the Lord had direct means of communicating with His people—visits from angels, prophetic dreams and visions, or the words and admonitions of the prophets.

> Enoch was a man of strong and highly cultivated mind and extensive knowledge; he was honored with special revelations from God. . . .
>
> Through holy angels God revealed to Enoch His purpose to destroy the world by a flood, and He also opened more fully to him the plan of redemption. By the spirit of prophecy He carried him down through the generations that should live after the Flood, and showed him the great events connected with the second coming of Christ and the end of the world.[2]

By rejecting the magic, divination, and sorcery of the nations around them, the Jews weren't coming up with something new. Instead, Israel was clinging to truths that reached back to Eden. Far from being novel and innovative, the Hebrew religion was actually a conservative holdover of truths that predated paganism. And it was this clinging—however feebly and sporadically—to this remnant truth that made them a remnant people.

---

1. Author's translation.
2. *Patriarchs and Prophets*, 85.

9

Of course, Israel didn't possess the remnant faith simply because it rejected polytheism, idolatry, and divination. The Jews possessed light that went back to the foundation of humanity, light that the pagans either didn't have at all or had greatly perverted.

In the first place, Israel kept the seventh-day Sabbath, which originated in Eden before the fall. "And God blessed the seventh day, and sanctified it: because that in it he had rested from all his work which God created and made" (Genesis 2:3). Thus, the seventh-day Sabbath was nothing new; actually, it was an old, lost truth that the Jews had recaptured and maintained.

Israel had the Ten Commandments in their pure form. Though the surrounding nations also had law codes, some of which reflect ideas in the Ten Commandments, none had what the Hebrews had in the Decalogue. Here, too, however, the Jews weren't given something new. The law existed all through patriarchal history and even before. Why was it wrong for Cain to kill Abel (see Genesis 4), or Abraham to lie (see Genesis 12), or Joseph to commit adultery with his master's wife (see Genesis 39), unless aspects of the law were already known? At Sinai, the Hebrews not only were given the law in a pure form, but were firmly admonished to keep it all, including the fourth commandment.

Israel had unique insights on the creation. Its pagan neighbors had all sorts of ridiculous stories—such as the *Enuma Elish* narrative, which taught that the earth was created as a result of a bitter battle between gods that began when certain gods disturbed the sleep of other gods. In contrast, the Jews believed the profound truths of Genesis, which

33

taught that God purposely made the earth and sky and then intimately created man out of the dust of the ground in His own image. By accepting the Genesis creation account, the Hebrews reached back and grasped the earliest and purest truths about creation.

Israel was given the sanctuary of the Lord and the unique message it taught. Though pagans, too, had sanctuaries and temples, the practices associated with them—prostitution and human sacrifice, for example—showed that these sanctuaries didn't teach what the Hebrew one did. The Jewish sanctuary was based on animal sacrifice, which the Bible traces back to Adam and Eve. Prior to the tabernacle in the wilderness, constructed after the establishment of the Sinai covenant (see Exodus 25:8), worshipers of the true God never sacrificed animals in a temple. They built altars instead, upon which they offered "burnt offerings" (Genesis 8:20). These burnt offerings remained the foundational sacrifice in the Hebrew sanctuary (see Exodus 29:38-42). Though the *form* itself was different—more elaborate and instructive than in earlier times—the essential truths taught by the sanctuary reflect truths taught by the first animal sacrificed outside Eden.

"In the divine planning," writes Frank Holbrook, "it was time for God's people to be given further insights into the nature of the Deity, the sin problem, and the means by which God would effect reconciliation with man, thereby restoring the harmonious union that the entrance of sin had ruptured. New light does not nullify old light. The essentials of *sacrifice* and *mediation* seen in the patriarchal age in the form of victim and father-priest are now elaborated upon in a new context: the tabernacle-temple sanctuary—the dwelling place of God."[1]

Unique among the peoples of the ancient world, the Hebrews also knew the truth about death. "In death there is no remembrance of thee: in the grave who shall give thee thanks?" (Psalm 6:5). They understood that, at death, man's "breath goeth forth, he returneth to his earth; in that very day his thoughts perish" (Psalm 146:4). Death, they understood, was a sleep: "David slept with his fathers, and was buried in the city of David" (1 Kings 2:10). This teaching differed radically from the understanding of death in the ancient world with its elaborate religious rituals and burial practices centered on the belief that the soul was immortal. Many Pharaohs spent years and untold riches building elaborate tombs for the great beyond. The literature of Israel's pagan neighbors is replete with stories about the afterlife.

Again, too, the truth about the state of the dead and the non-immortality of the soul goes back to Creation, when the Lord "formed man of the dust of the ground, and breathed into his nostrils the breath of life; and man *became* a living soul" (Genesis 2:7, emphasis supplied). The word for "soul," *nephesh*, is the same word used in the Creation account for animals: "And the Lord said, Let the earth bring forth the living creature [*nephesh*] after his kind, cattle, and creeping thing" (Genesis 1:24). At Creation the Lord taught that a soul is what we *are*, not something we possess until death. The Lord told Adam "dust thou art, and unto dust shalt thou return" (Genesis 3:19), an ancient truth that the Israelites understood, in stark contrast to the surrounding nations.

Israel also had a health message. Although the original diet in Eden was vegetarian (and the Israelites weren't), the distinction between clean and unclean foods, which the Jews adhered to, reaches back at least to Noah (see Genesis 7:2). The principle of a proper diet, however, can be found in Eden, when the Lord told our first parents what they were to eat (see Genesis 1:29). Here, too, the Hebrews were ahead of their neighbors, not because they had derived new truths, but because they had clung to old ones.

Also, the Hebrew nation had an understanding of the great controversy. Scattered about the Holy Scriptures was enough evidence to teach readers about the battle between God and Satan for the loyalty of man. The Book of Job, the oldest book of the Bible, clearly lays out the basic struggle between the Lord and Satan, one that began in heaven but is battled out on earth (see Job 1, 2). Other verses, such as Genesis 3:1-15, Ezekiel 28:12-15, and Isaiah 14:12-14 add insight to this important truth. Though the pagans had all sorts of ideas regarding good and evil, none had the understanding that the Jews did—again only because the Jews had ancient truths.

Israel also had the spirit of prophecy. During much of the nation's history, prophets, both canonical and noncanonical, had given specific messages, many of which were later included in the Bible. While its pagan neighbors looked into livers to discern the future, Isaiah proclaimed that "Cyrus . . . shall perform all my pleasure: even saying to Jerusalem, Thou shalt be built" (Isaiah 44:28)—a century and a half before the king and founder of the Persian Empire was born, much less fulfilled this prophetic utterance by freeing the Jews from Babylon and allowing them to rebuild. The Lord had been speaking through prophets and the prophetic gift all during the patriarchal era; Israel merely experienced an extension of the phenomenon.

Finally, Israel also enjoyed great light about the coming Redeemer, both His first and second advents, but particularly His first. The Jews were given the special privilege of announcing His arrival, and they themselves were to prepare for it (see Isaiah 42). Israel alone possessed the great prophecies of Isaiah 53, Daniel 9, Micah 5, and Psalm 22, and was to spread them to the world. Here, too, the teaching about the coming Redeemer was not new. Genesis 3:15, known as the *protevangelicum* (the first good news), has long been understood as the first Messianic promise. The Lord said to the serpent, "I will put enmity between . . . thy seed and her [the woman's] seed; it shall bruise thy head, and thou shalt bruise his heel."

The hope of a Redeemer goes back to our first parents. "Angels held communication with Adam after his fall and informed him of the plan of salvation and that the human race was not beyond redemption. Although a fearful separation had taken place between God and man, yet provision had been made through the offering of his beloved Son by which man might be saved."[2] Not only did the Jews have this ancient truth, which went back to Eden, but they were given even more light upon it than previous generations.

Israel, clearly, stood out from her pagan neighbors because of the truths that she alone possessed and the relationship she enjoyed with the true God. Moses told Israel:

> Behold, I have taught you statutes and judgments, even as the Lord my God commanded me, that ye should do so in the land whither ye go to possess it. Keep therefore and do them; for this is your wisdom and your understanding in the sight of the nations, which shall hear all these statutes, and say, Surely this great nation is a wise and understanding people. For what nation is there so great, who hath God so nigh unto them, as the Lord our God is in all things that we call upon him for? And what nation is there so great, that hath statutes and judgments so righteous as all this law, which I set before you this day? (Deuteronomy 4:5-8).

It was these—the laws and statutes, present truth, and the Jews' offer to obey them—that made the Hebrews a remnant people, adherents of truths lost since the beginning of the world, truths that they not only were to understand and obey, but to spread as well.

---

1. Frank Holbrook, "The Israelite Sanctuary," in *The Sanctuary and the Atonement*, ed. Arnold V. Wallenkampf and W. Richard Lesher (Washington, D.C.: General Conference of SDAs, 1981), 2.
2. *The Spirit of Prophecy*, 1:58, 59.

10

Unfortunately, from the making of the golden calf (see Exodus 32) to the stoning of Stephen (see Acts 7) fifteen hundred years later, the remnant never lived up to the truths given it. The gist of Scripture, especially the Old Testament, is not so much Israel's covenant calling, but its failure to abide by it.

Compromise with the pagans destroyed the nation during the First Temple Period. How often the prophets warned about Israel's fornication with the surrounding culture! Instead of elevating the pagans to its standard of righteousness, Israel absorbed and assimilated the beliefs and conduct of the pagans themselves.

Zephaniah warned about those who "worship the host of heaven upon the housetops; and them that worship and that swear by the Lord, and that swear by Malcham" (Zephaniah 1:5). Some Israelites worshiped the stars, a practice they learned from their neighbors, while others melded faith in the Lord with that of the Ammonite god, Malcham. They hadn't completely rejected their old religion; instead, they merely brought it up to date with contemporary thinking.

Ezekiel, in vision, saw paganism in the temple grounds—women "weeping for Tammuz" (Ezekiel 8:14) and even those who "worshipped the sun toward the east" (verse 16). The temple itself had "all the idols of the house of Israel, portrayed upon the wall round about" (verse 10). Again, the Israelites hadn't abandoned *all* their ancestral faith, but just enough to allow them to assimilate alien religious beliefs and practices into their own.

Because of their dalliance with those who didn't know the Lord, they lost their knowledge of Him as well. The Lord warned "there is no truth, nor mercy, nor the knowledge of God in the land" (Hosea 4:1). "For I desired mercy, not sacrifice; and the knowledge of God more than burnt offerings" (Hosea 6:6).

Nevertheless, the Jews believed that because they had "the truth," and because they were the special, chosen people of God—the "remnant," as it were—they would always be God's only faithful people. Jeremiah wrote about those who, despite sin and compromise, would come to the gates of the temple and say, "The temple of the Lord, the temple of the Lord, the temple of the Lord are these" (Jeremiah 7:4). No matter what they did, they believed they had the temple of God to save them.

Compromise and assimilation also caused them to be deceived with false concepts regarding righteousness and judgment. Many thought that God accepted them no matter what they did and that they would face no judgment: "Ye have wearied the Lord with your words. Yet ye say, Wherein have we wearied him? When ye say, Every one that doeth evil is good in the sight of the Lord, and he delighteth in them; or, Where is the God of judgment?" (Malachi 2:17).

Of course, Israel's religious perversions translated into moral and ethical ones as well. "The whole head is sick, And the whole heart faints. From the sole of the foot even to the head, There is no soundness in it, But wounds and bruises and putrefying sores" (Isaiah 1:5, 6, NKJV). Murder, adultery, thievery, incest, oppression, idolatry, fornication, envy, pride, lying—all the classic sins that God specifically warned about raged among them until the Lord cried out, "Hear the word of the Lord, ye rulers of Sodom; give ear unto the law of our God, ye people of Gomorrah. . . . I am full of the burnt offerings of rams, and the fat of fed beasts. . . . And when ye spread forth your hands, I will hide mine eyes from you: yea, when ye make many prayers, I will not hear" (Isaiah 1:10, 11, 15).

A major problem was that the Hebrew nation suffered from corrupt, vacillating, compromising leadership. Whether it was King Ahab and Queen Jezebel killing Naboth in order to get his vineyard (see 1 Kings 21), King Manasseh making Judah to do "worse than the heathen" (2 Chronicles 33:9), or the princes of Judah urging King Zedekiah to kill the prophet Jeremiah (see Jeremiah 38:4), a string of unfaithful, unconverted leaders brought the nation into one crisis after another until the whole house came tumbling down.

Many priests, too, the spiritual shepherds of the nation, apostatized. From the days of Nadab and Abihu who offered "strange fire" upon the altar (see Leviticus 10) until the final years of Judah, when Pashhur the priest struck Jeremiah and put him in stocks (see Jeremiah 20:2), false shepherds led the people astray. Zephaniah lamented that the "priests have polluted the sanctuary, they have done violence to the law" (Zephaniah 3:4); Isaiah warned about the priests who "have erred through strong drink, . . . they are swallowed up of wine" (Isaiah 28:7); and Ezekiel wrote: "Son of man, prophesy against the shepherds of Israel, prophesy, and say unto them, Thus saith the Lord God unto the shepherds; Woe be to the shepherds that do feed themselves! should not the shepherds feed the flocks?" (Ezekiel 34:2).

Israel's worship services became unacceptable to the Lord too. Malachi chided those who "offer the blind for sacrifice, is it not evil? and if ye offer the lame and the sick, is it not evil? offer it now unto thy governor; will he be pleased with thee, or accept thy person? saith the Lord of hosts" (Malachi 1:8). The Lord expressed His disgust with their worship: "Bring no more vain oblations; incense is an abomination unto me; the new moons and sabbaths, the calling of assemblies, I cannot away with; it is iniquity, even the solemn meeting" (Isaiah 1:13).

Deviation from the Word of God caused the nation to split into two kingdoms that sporadically warred against each other. Thus, when it should have been a united front, working out the Lord's will in spreading the truth to the world, God's chosen nation was so weakened with internal strife and bickering that it became easy prey for external enemies. After centuries of accommodating pagan practices, the Jews had no divine protection against pagan armies.

Remnant of the Remnant

11

Despite the capitulation, captivity, and eventual subjugation of Judah and Israel, the Lord promised to preserve a remnant. Mixed with the prophets' warnings of war, suffering, and ruin was their promise that a remnant would escape destruction and reestablish the nation.

> And it shall come to pass in that day, that the Lord shall set his hand again the second time to recover the *remnant* of his people, which shall be left, from Assyria, and from Egypt (Isaiah 11:11, emphasis supplied).

> And I will gather the *remnant* of my flock out of all the countries whither I have driven them, and will bring them again to their folds (Jeremiah 23:3, emphasis supplied).

> And I will lay the dead carcases of the children of Israel before their idols; and I will scatter your bones round about your altars. . . . Yet will I leave a *remnant*, that ye may have some that shall escape the sword among the nations, when ye shall be scattered through the countries (Ezekiel 6:5, 8, emphasis supplied).

The Lord kept His promises. Circumstances that should have ended the Jewish nation forever (its capital destroyed, its people either killed, left to languish, or taken captive)—didn't. Instead, the Lord brought back a remnant to the land to rebuild the temple and reestablish the nation. "And I will bring them, and they shall dwell in the midst of Jerusalem: and they shall be my people, and I will be their God, in truth and in righteousness" (Zechariah 8:8).

Unfortunately, this "remnant of the remnant" suffered from severe spiritual defects, not unlike the problems that had ruined their fathers a generation earlier. "The glowing picture," writes John Bright, "of the triumphant new exodus and the establishment of Yahweh's universal rule in Zion bore no resemblance to reality."[1]

First, despite Cyrus' liberal decree not only allowing the Jews to return to Jerusalem (see Ezra 1) but to rebuild the temple with funds out of his own treasury (see Ezra 6), many Jews were too comfortably assimilated in the foreign cultures, especially Babylon, to return. Seventy years after the first exiles returned, Ezra struggled to persuade Levites to leave Babylon and minister as priests in the new temple![2]

Second, when the new structure's foundation was complete, many of the older returnees—remembering the glory of Solomon's temple—wept over the new one's inferiority "until the people could not discern the noise of the shout of joy from the noise of the weeping" (Ezra 3:13). Their murmuring, complaining, and crying, wrote Ellen White, "had a depressing influence on the minds of many and weakened the hands of the builders."[3]

Also, the Samaritans "troubled them in building" (Ezra 4:4). This problem, along with the hardships of returning amid great poverty, so discouraged the people that the remnant quit the temple project for about fifteen years. Instead, they concentrated on their own homes. This attitude eventually brought the rebuke of the Lord, who withheld His blessings, "Because of mine house that is waste, and ye run every man unto his own house. Therefore the heaven over you is stayed from dew, and the earth is stayed from her fruit" (Haggai 1:9, 10).

Many of the remnant, including the spiritual leaders, married pagans, a practice that had brought the wrath of God upon their parents. Ezra, learning of these marriages, wrote, "I rent my garment and my mantle, and plucked off the hair of my head and of my beard, and sat down astonied" (Ezra 9:3). Eventually, the children of these heathen marriages couldn't even speak "in the Jews' language" (Nehemiah 13:24).

Wealthier members of the remnant took advantage of the poor by charging them usury until "there was a great cry of the people and of their wives against their brethren" (Nehemiah 5:1). Others uttered discouragement over the difficulties of building the city wall: "The strength of the bearers of burdens is decayed, and there is much rubbish; so that we are not able to build the wall" (Nehemiah 4:10). Some conspired with pagans to frustrate the work (see Nehemiah 6:10-12), while Eliashib the priest, "having the oversight of the chamber of the house of our God" (Nehemiah 13:4), actually let a pagan use the chamber as his own personal apartment! Many also did business on the Sabbath (see Nehemiah 13:15, 16).

Of course, sporadic repentance brought revival, and Israel eventually rebuilt the city and temple. Nevertheless, in light of the great promises regarding the Hebrew nation, this remnant failed in its spiritual mission, which was the center of its sacred covenant with Yahweh.

As time progressed, the situation worsened. Under Greek rule, which began in the fourth century B.C., the remnant quickly assimilated Hellenistic beliefs and customs. The Greeks established in Judea numerous *polioi*, cities that became the centers of Greek religion, culture, and government. Under the high priest Jason, who bought his position by bribing Greek ruler Antiochus IV, Jerusalem itself was converted into a *polis*, complete with a stadium where members of the remnant church, in the best Greek tradition, could compete in the nude (some even underwent painful operations to hide their circumcisions). In 172 B.C. another Jerusalem priest, Menelaus, robbed the temple treasury in an attempt to use the money to bribe Antiochus into making him high priest instead of Jason.

In response to later atrocities by Antiochus, who outlawed circumcision and Sabbath keeping and who offered idolatrous sacrifices on the altar, the Maccabees (also known as the Hasmoneans) waged a guerilla war that in three years successfully uprooted the enemy army from Jerusalem. The Hasmoneans, in about a decade, made Judea an independent state for the first time in more than four hundred years.

Unfortunately, this freedom didn't last long. The Romans, taking advantage of Hasmonean rulers fighting each other for power, captured Jerusalem in 63 B.C., and the Jews were again under a foreign yoke.

Thus, the corporate remnant "church," which should have conquered the pagan world with the gospel, found itself conquered by the pagan world instead. Given numerous chances to fulfill the covenant conditions, the remnant continually failed.

And, soon, it would face—and fail—the most important test of all.

---

1. Bright, 367.
2. See *Prophets and Kings*, 614, 615.
3. Ibid., 564.

12

I n the Old Testament, the great sin of Judah and Israel was accommodation with paganism; in New Testament times, the pendulum had swung to the other extreme. Afraid of being contaminated by foreign influences, the remnant church insulated itself until it became almost useless in the Lord's cause. Locked into such hard-nosed legalism, many of the covenant people rejected Jesus because He didn't fit their preconceived understanding of the "pillars," nor did He abide by their inviolable standards of righteousness and lifestyle.

The religious leaders' battles with Christ over the Sabbath exemplify this cold formalism. "This man is not of God," they said about Jesus, "because he keepeth not the Sabbath day" (John 9:16). So immersed were they in their rules, laws, and traditions that they missed the whole purpose of those rules, laws, and traditions. They were so cemented in a particular mind-frame that even Christ's miracles couldn't soften their attitudes. "Laying aside the commandment of God," Jesus told them, "ye hold the tradition of men, as the washing of pots and cups: and many other such like things" (Mark 7:8).

The Hebrew nation had become so obsessed with standards of righteousness—many of which were of their own devising and interpretation—that the standards became the ends instead of the means. Rather than seeing the law as part of their religion, the law alone became their religion. Thus, Israel had the commandments, but didn't know the Commandment-Giver; it heard about God's love, but didn't recognize that Love when it came in the flesh. It knew about salvation, but didn't know the Saviour; it was so obsessed with preserving truth that it didn't accept the Truth when He lived among them in person.

For the leaders, laws, standards, and rules mattered more than love, forgiveness, and tolerance. Concerned about protecting "historic Judaism," they rejected Christ because His teaching differed from their standards of holiness. They themselves could be caught up in the rankest sin and yet attack Someone who didn't follow their rules.

> Woe unto you, scribes and Pharisees, hypocrites! for ye pay tithe of mint and anise and cummin, and have omitted the weightier matters of the law, judgment, mercy, and faith: these ought ye to have done, and not to leave the other undone. Ye blind guides, which strain at a gnat, and swallow a camel (Matthew 23:23, 24).

Also, just like their fathers, who were certain that they were the elect of God and that nothing would change their status, the leaders in the time of Christ were convinced that *the synagogue would go through!* Because they were the literal seed of Abraham, the Hebrews believed that they would always be the "children of Abraham" in the spiritual, covenant sense. They

> cherished the idea that they were the favorites of heaven, and that they were always to be exalted as the church of God. They were the children of Abraham, they declared, and so firm did the foundation of their prosperity seem to them that they defied earth and heaven to dispossess them of their rights.[1]

Nevertheless, just before His death, Jesus overlooked the Holy City and cried,

> O Jerusalem, Jerusalem, thou that killest the prophets, and stonest them which are sent unto thee, how often would I have gathered thy children together, even as a hen gathereth her chickens under her wings, and ye would not! Behold, your house is left unto you desolate (Matthew 23:37, 38).

Of course, from the wilderness wanderings until Christ hung on the cross, many faithful Jews didn't partake of the apostasy. They refused,

Paul wrote, to bow "the knee to the image of Baal" (Romans 11:4), and these faithful ones existed all through Israel's history. In the time of Christ, and afterward, they would form the core of the new church. "Even so then," Paul said, "at this present time also there is a *remnant* according to the election of grace" (verse 5, emphasis supplied).

And these Jews, called into the *true* knowledge of God, would inaugurate the Christian church, which was itself the remnant of Israel.

---

1. *Christ's Object Lessons*, 294.

13

The New Testament writers saw the fledgling Christian community as a continuation of Israel, having acquired by faith in Christ the covenant promises made to Israel in the Old Testament: "And if ye be Christ's, then are ye Abraham's seed, and heirs according to the promise" (Galatians 3:29).

The writer of Hebrews quoted Jeremiah—"Behold, the days come, saith the Lord, when I will make a new covenant with the house of Israel and with the house of Judah" (Hebrews 8:8)—in the context of the New Testament church of Jews and Gentiles. Peter, echoing Old Testament imagery about national Israel, wrote to the Christians scattered throughout "Pontus, Galatia, Cappadocia, Asia, and Bithynia" (1 Peter 1:1) calling them "a chosen generation, a royal priesthood, an holy nation, a peculiar people" (1 Peter 2:9).

Thus, in every sense, the church became the new Israel, the new remnant. It took on the same functions, claimed the same promises, and had the same purpose as the old Israel, which was to teach the world about Yahweh, the Creator of the heavens and the earth, but now was to add a knowledge of the Son of God dying for the sins of the world. A major theme of the New Testament is the concept of a remnant of Jews and Gentiles called out of darkness into the light of Christ. Like the remnants that preceded it, this one would—through faith—accept the knowledge of the true God, a knowledge that went back to Eden itself, where the promise of the Messiah was first given (see Genesis 3:15). It was to preserve and spread ancient truths, except that now the New Testament church walked in the brilliant light of Jesus of Nazareth, the crucified and risen Saviour.

"The early Christians came to understand themselves, not as an exclusive remnant, but as an open universal remnant, no longer confined to the boundaries of Israel, but scattered all over the world."[1]

Unfortunately, this new remnant wasn't much different from those before it, even with the added knowledge that the Lord Himself came, suffered, and died as a sacrifice for sin. Paul wrote to one church, "It is reported commonly that there is fornication among you, and such fornication as is not so much as named among the Gentiles, that one should have *his father's wife*" (1 Corinthians 5:1). Ethnic bigotry (see Acts 6:1), even among the leaders (see Galatians 2:11-14), caused problems within the new remnant. Backsliders (see 2 Peter 2:19-22), false teachers (see 2 Peter 2:1), "busybodies" and "tattlers" (1 Timothy 5:13) contaminated the remnant church as well.

Theological disagreements plagued it, too, especially over law and grace. Acts 15:1, 2 reads: "And certain men which came down from Judaea taught the brethren, and said, Except ye be circumcised after the manner of Moses, ye cannot be saved. . . . therefore Paul and Barnabas had *no small dissension and disputation* with them" (emphasis supplied). In this case Paul and Barnabas were on the same side, yet in the same chapter these two leaders bitterly fought over a personnel issue:

> "And some days after Paul said unto Barnabas, Let us go again and visit our brethren in every city where we have preached the word of the Lord, and see how they do. And Barnabas determined to take with them John, whose surname was Mark. But Paul thought not good to take him with them, who departed from them from Pamphylia, and went not with them to the work. *And the contention was so sharp between them, that they departed asunder one from the other* (Acts 15:36-39, emphasis supplied).

False theology had crept in: "O foolish Galatians, who hath bewitched you, that ye should not obey the truth, before whose eyes Jesus Christ hath been evidently set forth, crucified among you?" (Galatians 3:1). In 2 Timothy 2:17 Paul warned, "And their word will eat as doth a canker: of whom is Hymenaeus and Philetus; Who concerning the truth have erred, saying that the resurrection is past already; and overthrow the faith of some."

Peter, talking about Paul's letters, warned: "As also in all his epistles, speaking in them of these things; in which are some things hard to be understood, which they that are unlearned and unstable wrest, as they do also the other scriptures, unto their own destruction" (2 Peter 3:16).

Of course, these problems were minuscule compared to what came later. Paul had warned about a great "falling away" (2 Thessalonians 2:3), and eventually the Christian church became so corrupt that it became the "antichristian" church instead. The Lord's true people went underground. "And the woman fled into the wilderness, where she hath a place prepared of God, that they should feed her there a thousand two hundred and threescore days" (Revelation 12:6).[2] Here, too, this remnant of believers—just like the patriarchs, ancient Israel, and the early Christians—attempted to cling to ancient truths amid mass apostasy.

Though persecution tended to purify the saints, these people had their defects too. The letters to the church during its underground sojourn, as well as when it resurfaced, make the problems apparent. The Lord told Pergamos to "repent" (Revelation 2:16); he warned Thyatira that "I have a few things against thee" (Revelation 2:20); and He said to Sardis, the Reformation church, that there were only "a few names even in Sardis which have not defiled their garments" (Revelation 3:4).

By the time of the Reformation, the reformed churches splintered into numerous groups that warred with each other when they weren't warring with Rome. Protestants killed each other by the thousands. Calvin burned his heretics; Zwingli drowned his; and Luther at one point urged that the state "smite, slay and stab, secretly or openly. . . as if among mad dogs" peasants who had revolted.

The Protestant churches all had major doctrinal errors as well. As time progressed, Protestant theology went in as many different directions as there were Protestant theologians. Predestination, once-saved-always-saved, antinomianism (no need of the law), infant baptism, the immortal soul, and an earthly millennium were just some of their teachings.

Churches swung from extreme scholasticism, in which religion was reduced to nothing but creeds, to extreme pietism, in which emotions and experience were the essence of true faith. Within a few centuries, rationalism, even denial of the supernatural, entered many denominations. Acceptance of evolution as the origin of all species did as well. Christians denied the deity of Christ and His preexistence before the incarnation. Others taught that Christ came again as a woman, or that after He left Palestine he went to the Americas. Some taught that once converted, a person could never sin. The Lord had to use Thomas Jefferson and James Madison, men distinctly outside the evangelical tradition, to retrieve from the Bible its principles of religious freedom, which were almost unknown among Protestants. Many churches sanctioned slavery as of God. Others began the slow drift back to Rome.

Of course, God had faithful people, and elements of pure biblical doctrines could still be found even though many different churches taught so many different things—many of them wrong. Basic truths that reached to the beginning of humanity's history, truths that the Lord's early people kept and promulgated, were either lost or so scattered that they were unavailable to the masses. Christianity, doctrinally, had gone deep into spiritual Babylon.

Therefore, as He had done thousands of years earlier, when His church was in literal Babylon, the Lord would again bring out a people who would recapture, restore, and promulgate those distinctive truths that went back to the beginning.

He would, again, call out a remnant.

---

1. Santo Calarco, "God's Universal Remnant," *Ministry*, August 1993, 6.
2. See also Revelation 12:14 and 13:15.

Remnant of
Her Seed

14

The next biblical remnant appears in Revelation 12 amid conflict, persecution, and deception. Within the first six verses, a woman travails "in birth" (verse 2); a dragon casts "the stars of heaven . . . to the earth" (verse 4) and then seeks to "devour her [the woman's] child" as soon as it is born (verse 4); and the woman flees "into the wilderness" (verse 6). In the next three verses there is a "war in heaven" (verse 7) in which the devil and his angels are cast out to the earth, where they deceive "the whole world" (verse 9). The next verses depict "the accuser of our brethren" (verse 10), then the martyrs who "loved not their lives unto the death" (verse 11), and the devil's "great wrath" (verse 12). The dragon then "persecuted the woman" (verse 13), and a serpent cast out of his mouth water "as a flood after the woman that he might cause her to be carried away" (verse 15). In the final verse, the dragon, angry with the woman, "went to make war with the remnant of her seed" (verse 17).

This chapter, obviously, isn't a day in the life of Bambi. Instead, using flashbacks (as so much of Revelation does), it sweeps over the history of the great controversy between Christ and Satan. Nowhere else in Scripture is the great controversy theme more graphically and succinctly described than in these seventeen verses. Thus, God's endtime remnant is introduced in the motif of the great controversy: "And the dragon was wroth with the woman, and went to make war with the remnant of her seed, which keep the commandments of God, and have the testimony of Jesus Christ" (verse 17).

Revelation 12:17, near the end of Scripture, is linked to a verse near the beginning, Genesis 3:15. After the fall, the Lord said to the serpent, who had just deceived Eve, "I will put enmity between thee [the serpent] and the woman, and between thy seed and her seed."

Revelation 12:17 and Genesis 3:15 parallel each other. Both deal with Satan, described not only as a dragon, but also as a serpent (see Revelation 12:9). Both depict the "woman" and "her seed"; and, while Genesis 3:15 talks about "enmity" between the woman (God's church)[1] and Satan—Revelation 12:17 says that Satan was "wroth" with the woman and made "war" against her seed. Here are the parallels between the two verses:

Genesis 3:15	Revelation 12:17
(1) Satan (serpent)	(1) Satan (dragon)
(2) woman	(2) woman
(3) woman's seed	(3) woman's seed
(4) enmity	(4) wrath, war

In actuality, Revelation 12:17 is Genesis 3:15 almost six thousand years later. The two stand like bookends around almost the entire Bible, which is—if anything—a description of the great controversy between Christ and Satan.

Who, then, is this "remnant of her seed," upon whom the dragon makes war?

A crucial factor in determining this identity is the time in which the remnant arises. In Revelation 12, the remnant appears, not only at the end of the vision itself, but also at the end of the chronological events depicted in that vision.

First was the war in heaven between Michael and His angels on the one hand and Satan and his angels on the other (see verses 7-9)—a war that resulted in Satan and his angels being cast down to the earth.

Then, the woman gives birth to a child, obviously Christ (see verse 5), who was born on the earth, where the dragon—cast out of heaven—was ready to "devour the child as soon as it was born" (verse 4; see also Matthew 2).

Next, the dragon attacks the woman: "And when the dragon saw that he was cast unto the earth, he persecuted the woman which brought forth the man child" (verse 13).

As a result of this attack, the woman, God's church, is twice depicted as fleeing into the wilderness: "And the woman fled into the wilderness, where she hath a place prepared of God, that they should feed her there a thousand two hundred and threescore days" (verse 6). "And to the woman were given two wings of a great eagle, that she might fly into the wilderness, into her place, where she is nourished for a time, and times, and half a time, from the face of the serpent" (verse 14).

Finally, following this time period in which the woman fled into the wilderness, the remnant is introduced: "And the dragon was wroth with the woman, and went to make war with the remnant of her seed, which keep the commandments of God, and have the testimony of Jesus Christ" (verse 17).

The first characteristic of the remnant, then, is that it must come *after* the time period when the woman fled into the wilderness, the "time, times, and half a time" (verse 14) or the "thousand two hundred and threescore days" (verse 6).

"The vision makes clear that *after* the 1260 days/three and a half times," writes William Johnsson, "the dragon will concentrate its efforts on the woman's descendants."[2]

Because a "time" is translated year, "times" two years, and "half a time" half a year—"times, time, and half a time" is three and a half years, or, according to Revelation 12:6, "a thousand two hundred and threescore days" (1260 days). Because both verses depict the same event, the woman fleeing into the wilderness from the dragon, the time frame in both verses must be the same.

The persecution of the saints in Daniel 7 unlocks the time frame of Revelation 12:6, 14. Daniel dreamed of four beasts. The first, "like a lion" (Daniel 7:4), was Babylon; the second, "like to a bear" (verse 5), was Medo-Persia; the third, "like a leopard" (verse 6), was Greece; and the fourth, "dreadful and terrible, and strong exceedingly" (verse 7), was pagan Rome. This fourth beast had "ten horns," a parallel to the ten-horned dragon of Revelation 12:3, which was also Rome in its pagan stage. Thus Daniel 7 and Revelation 12 are clearly linked. According to Matthew, pagan Rome (via Herod) attempted to "devour" the woman's child, Christ, "as soon as it was born."

In the vision of Daniel 7, a powerful little horn with "eyes like the eyes of man, and a mouth speaking great things" (verse 8) arose out of pagan Rome. This little-horn power, which was not separate from the fourth beast (Rome), but part of it, "made war with the saints, and prevailed against them" (verse 21) for "a time and times and half a time" (verse 25)—the same period that the woman of Revelation 12, God's church, fled into the wilderness from the dragon, which persecuted (or "made war with") her. Obviously, both Daniel and Revelation are referring to the same event. The Septuagint, an early Greek translation of the Hebrew Bible, used the same basic phrase in Daniel 7:25 that John did in Revelation 12:14. Because so much of Revelation borrows from the Old Testament, John probably took the phrase directly from Daniel 7:25 itself.[3]

The little horn, then, must be Rome too, though now in its papal stage. And the "time, times and half a time" of Daniel 7:25 and Revelation 12:14 both depict the period of papal Rome's persecution of the "saints of the most high," or "the woman." The dragon used Rome, in its pagan phase, to attempt to kill Christ (Revelation 12:4); and he used Rome again, in its papal phase, to attack the Lord's church (verses 6 and 14).

When is the specific time period of that attack?

In Daniel 7, symbolic beasts are doing symbolic things in a symbolic time frame. A "time, times, and half a time" is not a common way to delineate time, any more than is "a thousand two hundred and three-score days." Why didn't the prophet just say "three-and-a-half years" if he meant a literal three-and-a-half years? Instead, the prophecy demands—as many commentators have believed through the centuries—the day-year principle, which means that the "time, times, and half a time" and the "one thousand two hundred and three score days" are actually delineating 1260 years.[4]

Adventist commentators have defined the starting point of the prophecy as A.D. 538, when the papacy drove out the last Arian power from Rome, and A.D. 1798 as its end, when the French took the pope captive.[5] However, these exact dates aren't requisite for the prophecy to be understood. Instead, two simple points, firmly established in Scripture, will do. First, the persecution both in Daniel 7 and Revelation 12:6, 14 came from papal Rome. Second, the day-year principle is applied to their time prophecies. With these two prophetic axioms, the first characteristic of the remnant becomes clear.

Papal Rome became established in the sixth century A.D. Twelve hundred and sixty years later brings us at least to the late eighteenth or early nineteenth century. Therefore, only *after* that specific period does the "remnant of her seed" first appear. Thus, it is *after* the late eighteenth or early nineteenth century, when the 1260 years end and the remnant first appears.

Though the prophetic time frame, in and of itself, doesn't show who the remnant is, it does show who it isn't. Because the remnant can appear only after the 1260-year period, somewhere after the late eighteenth or early nineteenth century, all the major Reformation churches are automatically eliminated. Though people from these bodies can and do and will become part of the remnant, these denominations as corporate entities arose directly out of the Reformation, which was in the sixteenth and seventeenth centuries—too early to be "the remnant of her seed." Lutherans, Methodists, Baptists, Seventh Day Baptists, Episcopalians, Presbyterians, Congregationalists, all have been around too long to be, *in any corporate sense*, the remnant depicted in Revelation 12:17. "The remnant of her seed" must come sometime *after* the 1260-year period, *after* the late eighteenth or early nineteenth century.

The identification of the remnant, however, can't end here. Many divergent church bodies arose after the 1260-year period. More details are needed to identify the remnant, and, fortunately, more are given.

The second characteristic of the "remnant of her seed" is that "they keep the commandments of God" (Revelation 12:17). Whatever construction people want to put on the phrase "the commandments of God," it must surely mean *at least* (if nothing else), the Ten Commandments.

• Here is the patience of the saints: here are they that keep the commandments of God, and the faith of Jesus (Revelation 14:12).

• He that saith, I know him, and keepeth not his commandments, is a liar, and the truth is not in him (1 John 2:4).

• Do we then make void the law through faith? God forbid: yea, we establish the law (Romans 3:31).

• Honour thy father and mother; which is the first commandment with promise (Ephesians 6:2).

• Blessed are they that do his commandments, that they may have right to the tree of life, and may enter in through the gates into the city (Revelation 22:14).

• If ye love me, keep my commandments (John 14:15).

Of course, included in God's commandments—even at their heart—is the fourth, which is neglected by almost the whole Christian world. Even many who claim to keep it, don't, because most observe the first day of the week instead of the seventh. No matter how sincerely, earnestly, and diligently a person may be in his observance of Sunday, the Bible says that "the seventh day"—not the first—"is the sabbath of the Lord thy God" (Exodus 20:10). Thus, in order to fit the second characteristic of the remnant, one must be keeping God's commandments—including the Sabbath commandment.

"For whoever shall keep the whole law, and yet stumble in one point, he is guilty of all. For He who said, '*Do not commit adultery*,' also said, '*Do not murder*.' Now if you do not commit adultery, but you do murder, you have become a transgressor of the law" (James 2:10, 11, NJKV, emphasis supplied). James could just as easily have written, "For he who said, 'Do not commit adultery' also said, 'Remember the Sabbath day.' Now if you do not commit adultery, but ye do not remember the Sabbath day, you have become a transgressor of the law."

The importance of the Sabbath becomes clearer in Revelation 14. In the context of the last days, an angel—using language directly from the Sabbath commandment—calls upon the inhabitants of the earth to "worship him that made heaven, and earth, and the sea, and the fountains of waters" (Revelation 14:7), in contrast to those who "worship the beast and his image" (verse 9). In the midst of this conflict over worship, God's people are described as those who "keep the commandments of God, and the faith of Jesus" (Revelation 14:12). Here, as in Revelation 12:17, the commandments of God are given prominence—and, of all the commandments, only the fourth deals specifically with the worship of the Lord as the One who "made heaven, and earth, and the sea." No doubt, then, that when Revelation talks about the remnant, which keeps "the commandments of God," the fourth is included.

   This second identifying mark, then, eliminates the vast majority of those not eliminated by the first. Many church bodies, such as Pentecostals, Mormons, Jehovah's Witnesses, and others, arose after the 1260-year period, but almost all reject the fourth commandment, either by keeping no day or the wrong day. The commandments of God must include the seventh-day Sabbath; therefore, the "remnant of her seed," besides arising after the late eighteenth or early nineteenth century, will be seventh-day Sabbath keepers as well.

   Thus, with this second characteristic, the options for the remnant have been greatly narrowed. Fortunately, another trait remains, one which pares down the field to a positive identification. Revelation 12:17 teaches that this remnant would also have "the testimony of Jesus Christ."

---

1. Throughout Scripture the Lord uses the image of a woman to describe His church. See Isaiah 26:17; 54:5; 65:2; 66:7-9; Jeremiah 2:2; Jeremiah 3:14; 6:2-4; Micah 4:10; Hosea 2:19, 20; 2 Corinthians 11:1; Revelation 21:2.
2. William Johnsson, "The Saints' End-Time Victory Over the Forces of Evil," in *Symposium on Revelation*, ed. Frank Holbrook (Silver Spring, Md.: Biblical Research Institute, 1992), 18.
3. This evidence for the borrowing becomes even more likely when one looks at the next chapter, chapter 13, which is clearly based on the vision of Daniel 7.
4. See also Clifford Goldstein, *1844 Made Simple* (Boise, Idaho: Pacific Press, 1989); William Shea, *Selected Studies on Prophetic Interpretation* (Takoma Park, Md.: General Conference of SDAs, 1982).
5. For more details, see Mervyn Maxwell, *God Cares* (Boise, Idaho: Pacific Press, 1981), 2:328, 329.

15

Early in His earthly ministry, Jesus stood before a crowd and spoke about John the Baptist. After quoting Scripture that He applied to John, Jesus said: "For I say unto you, Among those that are born of women there is not a greater prophet than John the Baptist" (Luke 7:28).

These words have profound importance in understanding the meaning of "the testimony of Jesus" (Revelation 12:17), the final identification mark of God's end-time remnant.

How?

If, until Christ's time, no greater prophet than John existed, then the prophet Amos, for example, could be only less than or equal to John, but not greater. Jeremiah, as a prophet, was either less than or, at best, equal to John—but not greater. King David, too, was either John's inferior or at most his equal, but not his superior. Even Isaiah and Moses, as great as they were, couldn't be greater than John because, as Jesus Himself said, "There is not a greater prophet than John the Baptist."

Although Jesus didn't specify the reason for John's greatness, more than likely it was because John stood as the forerunner to the Messiah Himself; no other prophet had had that privilege. The special sacredness of John's divine call, perhaps, entitled him to this preeminent position.

Whatever the reason for John's status, a significant difference exists between him and these other prophets—a difference that has nothing to do with his status, but that clearly differentiates John's prophetic calling from that of the others.

What was that difference?

John the Baptist has no writings in the Bible!

Christ's words about John prove two points: first, one doesn't have to be canonical (have his or her writings placed in Scripture) to be a prophet; and, second, one doesn't have to be canonical to be a great prophet.

The Bible attests to several full-fledged, card-carrying prophets who never wrote anything that was included in it. After having impregnated a soldier's wife and then having that soldier murdered so he could keep the woman for himself, David was confronted by Nathan (named a prophet in 2 Samuel 7:2), who declared: "Thou art the man" (2 Samuel 12:7). And yet Nathan wrote nothing that was placed in the Bible.

Elijah, the prophet, (see 2 Chronicles 21:12), stood before Ahab, king of Israel, and said: "As the Lord God of Israel liveth, before whom I stand, there shall not be dew nor rain these years, but according to my word" (1 Kings 17:1). Here, too, is a prophet of no little authority, yet he had no writings canonized either.

What about "the prophet Gad" (1 Samuel 22:5), who helped David in his flight from Saul, or "the prophet Ahijah the Shilonite" (1 Kings 11:29), who prophesied about the breakup of the Jewish nation, or "Shemaiah the prophet" (2 Chronicles 12:5) or "the prophet Iddo" (2 Chronicles 13:22) or "Oded the prophet" (2 Chronicles 15:8) or "Elisha the prophet" (2 Kings 6:12)? Though some of these prophets even wrote books, none ever made it into Scripture.

In the days of the judges, the Hebrew nation was subdued by the Canaanite king, Jabin, who for twenty years "mightily oppressed the children of Israel" (Judges 4:3). When time for deliverance came, to whom did the people go for guidance, assurance, and leadership? To "Deborah, a prophetess" (verse 4), who gave Israel instruction and even went to the battlefield herself in order to encourage the troops. Not only did Deborah have no book in the Bible, but this prophet was a woman!

After King Josiah of Judah listened to the reading of "the book of the law" (2 Kings 22:11), he said, "Go ye, enquire of the Lord for me, and for the people, and for all Judah, concerning the words of this book that is found: for great is the wrath of the Lord that is kindled against us" (verse 13). In obedience to the king's command, his servants went to "Huldah the prophetess" (verse 14), who said: "Thus saith the Lord, Behold, I will bring evil upon this place, and upon the inhabitants thereof, even all the words of the book which the king of Judah hath read" (verse 16).

This phenomenon—a woman prophet—occurs not only in the Old Testament, but also in the New. After Jesus was born, his parents took Him to the Jerusalem temple to be dedicated. Among those present at His dedication was "Anna, a prophetess, the daughter of Phanuel, of the tribe of Aser" (Luke 2:36). She came into the temple grounds at the time Simeon uttered a prophecy to Mary regarding the baby Jesus, and Anna the prophetess also prophesied: "In that instant [she] gave thanks likewise unto the Lord, and spake of him to all them that looked for redemption in Jerusalem" (verse 38). Anna, too, had no writings in the Bible.

Luke writes about "Philip the evangelist" (Acts 21:8) in Caesarea, who "had four daughters, virgins, which did prophesy" (verse 9). None of their prophecies ever made it into the canon either.

Scripture proves that not only did the Lord use prophets who had no writings in the Bible, but that some of these prophets were—women!

Prophecy is clearly a New Testament phenomenon, as well as an Old Testament one. Paul wrote:

> Wherefore he saith, When he ascended up on high, he led captivity captive, and gave gifts unto men. . . . And he gave some, apostles; and *some*, *prophets*; and some, evangelists; and some, pastors and teachers; *For the perfecting of the saints*, for the work of the ministry, for the edifying of the body of Christ: Till we all come in *the unity of the faith*, and of the knowledge of the Son of God, unto a perfect man, unto the measure of *the stature of the fulness of Christ* (Ephesians 4:8, 11-13, emphasis supplied).

Obviously, the saints are a long way from their "perfecting"; obviously, their stature is not yet "the fulness of Christ"; obviously, the church hasn't yet come "into the unity of the faith." Yet these ideals are the goals of the gifts. Why, therefore, would they be withdrawn from the church before accomplishing their task? Also, pastors, teachers, and even apostles (those who raise up churches) still exist, so why not prophets as well?

Paul also wrote that "in every thing ye are enriched by him, in all utterance, and in all knowledge; Even as the testimony of Christ was confirmed in you: So that ye come behind in no gift; waiting for the coming of our Lord Jesus Christ" (1 Corinthians 1:5-7). Paul wanted the church, which was waiting for the coming of the Lord, to be behind in no gift, which must have included the gift of prophecy: "And God hath set some in the church, first apostles, secondarily prophets, thirdly teachers" (1 Corinthians 12:28).

In a response to a question about the signs of His second coming, Jesus told His followers that in the last days, "many false prophets shall arise, and shall deceive many" (Matthew 24:11). He didn't say, "Beware of anyone who claims to be a prophet, because there will be no more prophets." On the contrary, His warning about false prophets implies the presence of true ones, even near the end of the world.

And, finally, the description of God's end-time remnant also teaches that prophecy will be manifested in the last days: "And the dragon was wroth with the woman, and went to make war with the remnant of her seed, which keep the commandments of God, and have *the testimony of Jesus Christ*" (Revelation 12:17, emphasis supplied).

What is "the testimony of Jesus Christ"?

Scholars disagree on whether "the testimony of Jesus Christ" means the general testimony of the Christian church regarding Jesus (their witness), or whether it is the testimony that Jesus Himself bears through the prophetic gift.[1] However, a parallel verse helps prove that the latter meaning is correct—that "the testimony of Jesus" is the testimony Jesus Himself bears: "Then I fell down at his feet to worship him [the angel], but he said to me, 'You must not do that! I am a fellow servant with you and your brethren who hold the testimony of Jesus. Worship God.' *For the testimony of Jesus is the spirit of prophecy*" (Revelation 19:10, RSV).

The "testimony of Jesus" then, is obviously manifested as the spiritual gift of prophecy. Revelation 22:8, 9 helps clarify the meaning even more:

Revelation 19:10 (RSV)	Revelation 22:8-9 (RSV)
Then I fell down at his feet to worship him,	I fell down to worship at the feet of the angel who showed them to me;
but he said to me, "You must not do that! I am a fellow servant with you and your brethren who hold *the testimony of Jesus.* Worship God." For the testimony of Jesus is the spirit of prophecy.	but he said to me, "You must not do that! I am a fellow servant with you and *your brethren the prophets,* and with those who keep the words of this book. Worship God."

In both passages, John falls at the feet of the angel to worship him, and in both places the angel's responses are almost identical. Yet one difference is significant. In Revelation 19:10 the brethren are identified by the phrase, "who hold [the Greek really means "have"] the testimony of Jesus." In 22:9, the brethren are simply called the "prophets." This comparison shows that "the testimony of Jesus," which is "the spirit of prophecy," is the prophetic gift given to the prophets. Prophets have "the spirit of prophecy."

Jews in John's day would have understood the phrase "the spirit of prophecy" as either the Holy Spirit in a general sense, or more specifically as the Spirit given to the prophets. J. P. Schafer writes about ancient postbiblical Jewish writings: "In other words, the term 'Spirit of Prophecy' describes a clearly delineated situation, namely, the Holy Spirit sent from God who imparts the prophetic gift to man."[2] F. F. Bruce writes, "The expression 'the spirit of prophecy' is current in post-biblical Judaism: it is used, for example, in Targumic circumlocution for the Spirit of Yahweh which comes upon this or that prophet."[3]

Thus, "the remnant of her seed" (Revelation 12:17), the final biblical remnant, will not only arise after the late eighteenth or early nineteenth century; it will not only keep all the commandments of God, including the fourth; but it will have the "spirit of prophecy," the prophetic gift. Prophecy *must* be manifest among it, because "the spirit of prophecy" is one of three major identifying marks of the remnant.

In this context, the following excerpt from *Early Writings* becomes relevant:

> The Lord has given me a view of other worlds. Wings were given me, and an angel attended me from the city to a place that was bright and glorious. The grass of the place was living green, and the birds there warbled a sweet song. The inhabitants of the place were of all sizes; they were noble, majestic, and lovely. They bore the express image of Jesus, and their countenances beamed with holy joy, expressive of the freedom and happiness of the place. I asked one of them why they were so much more lovely than those on the earth. The reply was, "We have lived in strict obedience to the commandments of God, and have not fallen by disobedience, like those on the earth." Then I saw two trees, one looked much like the tree of life in the city. The fruit of both looked beautiful, but of one they could not eat. . . . Then I was taken to a world which had seven moons. There I saw good old Enoch, who had been translated. On his right arm he bore a glorious palm, and on each leaf was written "Victory." Around his head was a dazzling white wreath, and leaves on the wreath, and in the middle of each leaf was written "Purity," and around the wreath were stones of various colors. . . . I asked him if this was the place he was taken to from the earth. He said, "It is not; the city is my home, and I have come to visit this place." He moved about the place as if perfectly at home. I begged of my attending angel to let me remain in that place. I could not bear the thought of coming back to this dark world again.[4]

What do you do with this? Her words leave only a few options as to their origin. Either this woman was a demonically inspired fraud, a lunatic, or she manifested "the spirit of prophecy." Either she was one of the greatest deceivers in the history of Christianity or one of its greatest prophets. Someone who claims that in vision she was taken to other worlds and spoke to inhabitants on them is either lying, a crazed charlatan, or a prophet through whom the Lord has opened vistas of light and truth unlike anything else the world has witnessed since apostolic days.

The same principle is true of Christ. Some have viewed Him merely as a great prophet. Yet a great prophet isn't going to say, "I am the way, the truth, and the life: no man cometh unto the Father, but by me" (John 14:6), or "I am the resurrection, and the life: he that believeth in me, though he were dead, yet shall he live" (John 11:25). Either He was a liar or a lunatic or He was indeed the Way and the Truth and the Life and the Resurrection. How can there be any middle ground?

Ellen White leaves only similar options. Her work doesn't afford us the luxury of compromise. No one need claim that the woman was infallible, perfect, or did not need growth or correction. No one need claim that her writings are on par with the Bible or that they should be the ultimate standard of truth. And no one can deny that her writings have been abused by some who believe them.

Yet what are we to conclude when she describes scenes in detail, as she does in this account of Pilate's wife's dream?

> She saw Him [Jesus] on trial in the judgment hall. She saw the hands tightly bound as the hands of a criminal. She saw Herod and his soldiers doing their dreadful work. . . . She saw the cross uplifted on Calvary. She saw the earth wrapped in darkness, and heard the mysterious cry, "It is finished." Still another scene met her gaze. She saw Christ seated upon the great white cloud, while the earth reeled in space, and His murderers fled from the presence of His glory.[5]

Such detail means either that she was describing what was shown to her through the spirit of prophecy, or that she was a deceiver perpetrating one of the greatest spiritual deceptions since Joseph Smith's magic glasses supposedly enabled him to translate the golden tablets into the *Book of Mormon*.

Who gave Ellen White insight regarding Abraham's call to sacrifice Isaac on Mount Moriah? Where did she learn that "with trembling voice, Abraham unfolded to his son the divine message"? How did she know that Isaac "felt that he was honored in being called to give his life as an offering to God"? What spirit inspired her to write that Isaac "tenderly seeks to lighten the father's grief, and encourages his nerveless hands to bind the cords that confine him to the altar"?[6] Was all this from the devil?

How does one explain the source for her description of this scene in heaven after the resurrection of the saints?

As the ransomed ones are welcomed to the City of God, there rings out upon the air an exultant cry of adoration. The two Adams are about to meet. The Son of God is standing with outstretched arms to receive the father of our race—the being whom He created, who sinned against his Maker, and for whose sin the marks of the crucifixion are borne upon the Saviour's form. As Adam discerns the prints of the cruel nails, he does not fall upon the bosom of his Lord, but in humiliation casts himself at His feet, crying: "Worthy, worthy is the Lamb that was slain!" Tenderly the Saviour lifts him up and bids him look once more upon the Eden home from which he has so long been exiled.[7]

What inspired these insights on the resurrection of Christ?

A mighty angel came flying swiftly from heaven. His face was like the lightning, and his garments white as snow. His light dispersed the darkness from his track and caused the evil angels, who had triumphantly claimed the body of Jesus, to flee in terror from his brightness and glory. One of the angelic host who had witnessed the scene of Christ's humiliation, and was watching His resting place, joined the angel from heaven, and together they came down to the sepulcher. The earth trembled and shook as they approached, and there was a great earthquake. . . . As the light of the angels shone around, brighter than the sun, that Roman guard fell as dead men to the ground. One of the angels laid hold of the great stone and rolled it away from the door of the sepulcher and seated himself upon it. The other entered the tomb and unbound the napkin from the head of Jesus. Then the angel from heaven, with a voice that caused the earth to quake, cried out, "Thou Son of God, Thy Father calls Thee! Come forth."[8]

Ellen White declared that her writings "either bear the signet of God or that of Satan."[9] Which one inspired the preceding descriptions?

No doubt some have taken her writings out of context to prove points she wouldn't agree with. No doubt those on all sides of any argument—whether over the nature of Christ or the medicinal value of cayenne pepper—pile up quotes from her to prove their positions. No doubt her writings have been used to beat people over the head until they can no longer stand to read her. No doubt some exalt her writings to such a level that they have caused many to all but discard them due to false expectations and notions of her inspiration. No doubt some get their doctrines from Ellen White and not from the Bible. No doubt for some she is the final authority on everything. No doubt that her writings have been misused, abused, and twisted in a hundred other ways. *But none of these problems should mitigate against the gift!*

No doubt.

---

1. See Gerald Pfandl, "The Remnant Church and the Spirit of Prophecy," in *Symposium on Revelation*, ed. Frank Holbrook (Silver Spring, Md.: Biblical Research Institute, 1992), 2:303-322.
2. Quoted in *Symposium on Revelation*, 6:317.
3. Ibid., 318.
4. *Early Writings*, 39, 40.
5. *The Desire of Ages*, 732.
6. See *Patriarchs and Prophets*, 152.
7. *The Great Controversy*, 647.
8. *Early Writings*, 181, 182.
9. *Testimonies to the Church*, 5:98.

16

With this final characteristic, identification of the remnant becomes certain. Let's review Revelation 12:17, plugging in the information we have found:

And the dragon [Satan] was wroth with the woman [God's church], and went to make war with the remnant of her seed [who must appear only after the late eighteenth or early nineteenth century], which keep the commandments of God [including the seventh-day Sabbath], and have the testimony of Jesus Christ [the spirit of prophecy revealed in the ministry of Ellen G. White].

Could it be just a coincidence, too, that among the handful of groups who fit the first two characteristics of the end-time remnant, only one has the third characteristic, the "spirit of prophecy," powerfully present within it? This three-fold specification corroborates the identification of God's end-time remnant with the Seventh-day Adventist Church.

But how could the Seventh-day Adventist Church be that remnant? How could a movement troubled by so much turmoil, dissension, and bickering be the remnant? Can a cold, dead, asleep church be the remnant? Or one filled with legalism, worldliness, divorce, adultery, and sexual misconduct? Or one that doesn't live up to the standards the Lord has given it? Or one that has made those standards alone its religion? Or that argues over almost every doctrine? Can a body tainted with corruption, who neglects prophetic guidance, and who has some members advocating various heresies, be the remnant?

Of course it can!

Look at ancient Israel. For more than a thousand years, it remained God's remnant despite being guilty of every sin under the sun. Scripture weeps with the failings, heresies, and apostasies of the Old Testament remnant. Corruption, bickering, compromise, adultery, legalism, hypocrisy, heresies—all existed in the remnant in past ages, just as they do today. *And yet none of these things nullified its remnant status!*

Even after centuries of apostasy, corruption, sin, decadence, and evil, national Israel remained God's remnant people. Only after the Lord called out another group (the Christian church), which had accepted greater light than national Israel, did the Hebrew nation, corporately and politically, lose its remnant role.

The remnant, as a corporate entity, has never been defined exclusively by the holiness of its members, but rather by the advanced light it possessed. From those who entered the boat with Noah, up through the Protestant Reformation, the corporate remnant has been defined more by the light it has possessed than by the holiness of those who possessed that light—if for no other reason than that many of those who had the light were *not* holy.

Until the first coming of Christ and the formation of the Christian church, for example, Israel had a fuller revelation of the Lord than did any other religion. No matter how corrupt the nation had become, no matter how far it had deviated from God's will—either under the compromise of the First Temple Period, or the self-righteous legalism of the second—Israel still had far more light than its pagan neighbors. Israel had present truth, and that truth, more than anything else, defined its remnant status.

It is the same with Adventism. No matter how much hypocrisy, compromise, sin, and apostasy there may be in this movement, it has been blessed with a fuller revelation of Christ and of present truth than any other corporate faith. Never mind that many members are not following that light (they didn't in Israel), or that these truths aren't sanctifying many (they didn't in Israel), or that these truths aren't appreciated (they weren't in Israel), or that the nasty and unconverted give the message a bad name at every turn (they did in Israel as well). What's crucial is that the Seventh-day Adventist Church, like ancient

Israel, has been given far more light than any other faith, and that light alone gives it corporate remnant status.

If a Jew living in Israel at any period prior to Christianity had become discouraged because of the sin, bickering, and coldness of the Hebrew faith, where would he go? If he were sickened by the degradation, the worldliness, the compromise that permeated the Hebrew nation in the First Temple Period; or if he were oppressed and discouraged by the right-wing dogmatism and hypocricy of the Second Temple Period, where would he go? To Roman sun-worship? To Egyptian frog-worship? To the great mystery cults? Would he join the religion of Diana? Or the Canaanite cult of Baal? No matter how sorry a state his church was in, he wouldn't find more doctrinal truth elsewhere.

It's the same with Adventism today. Where could a disgruntled Adventist go without compromising his most basic beliefs? To a church that keeps Sunday instead of the biblical Sabbath? Or one that believes the dead are now burning in hell? Once those two doctrines are eliminated, the alternatives get painfully slim.

Indeed, an Adventist seeking to leave Adventism today would face problems similar to those a Jew in Bible times would have faced seeking to leave Judaism. Of course, the doctrinal distinctions between Adventist Christians and other Protestants (or even between Adventists and Roman Catholics or members of non-Christian religions) is not as great as was the distinction between the doctrines of ancient Israel and those of the surrounding nations. Yet the distinctions are clear enough that any reasonably well-informed Adventist should realize that no viable doctrinal alternative exists.

For example, millions of Christians "speak in tongues," proof, they believe, of the indwelling Holy Spirit. These unintelligible noises are supposed to be a modern manifestation of the spiritual gift received at Pentecost, when the Holy Spirit fell upon the apostles and they "began to speak with other tongues, as the Spirit gave them utterance" (Acts 2:4).

According to the book of Acts, however, the Pentecostal gift of tongues enabled the recipients to speak in foreign languages (see Acts 2:11), a vastly different phenomenon from the pandemonium of some charismatic Pentecostal worship today.

Something's wrong, too, with a phenomenon that almost universally ignores Paul's warning against everyone in the congregation speaking in tongues all at once: "If therefore the whole church be come together into one place, and all speak with tongues, and there come in those that are unlearned, or unbelievers, will they not say that ye are mad?" (1 Corinthians 14:23). Every Sunday all over the world, whole churches—sometimes hundreds if not thousands of worshipers—"speak in tongues" at the same time, despite Paul's words that "If any man speak in an unknown tongue, let it be by two, or at the most by three, and that by course; and let one interpret" (verse 27).

No doubt, many charismatics are earnest, sincere Christians who know and love the Lord and whose names are written in the book of life. Even if the "gifts" are questionable, many manifest in their lives the *fruits* of the Spirit—and to a greater degree than some Adventists. No doubt, too, many charismatics will be in God's kingdom, while many Adventists won't, even with the added light that comes from Ellen White's warning about those who "have an unmeaning gibberish which they call the unknown tongue, which is unknown not only by man but by the Lord and all heaven."[1]

Far from preparing a people for the second coming, the "tongues" movement has been in the forefront of those uniting Catholics and Protestants in what will ultimately coalesce into the apostate religious system that persecutes God's commandment-keeping people.

Another teaching, more dangerous than "tongues," is the doctrine of "eternal security," commonly known as "once saved, always saved." As implausible as it might seem, millions believe that once a person has accepted Christ as his personal Saviour, then nothing that person can do will jeopardize his salvation. He is eternally sealed by Christ's blood, and no matter the character he develops or the depths of sin he reaches, this person is assured of eternal life.

In contrast, Jesus Himself warned "he that endureth to the end shall be saved" (Matthew 10:22). Paul admonished believers to "work out your own salvation with fear and trembling" (Philippians 2:12). Paul said, too, "I keep under my body, and bring it into subjection: lest that by any means, when I have preached to others, I myself should be a castaway" (1 Corinthians 9:27). Though Christians can, and should, have assurance of salvation, the doctrine of "once saved, always saved" carries that assurance to an absurd degree.

I don't judge the sincerity, faith, or Christian experience of those who believe it, but this teaching is not truth, much less present truth. On the contrary, how difficult it will be for anyone, facing the crisis of the end, to decide to be faithful to the "commandments of God" if he is convinced that because he has accepted Christ, no subsequent choice or decision can cause him to lose his salvation. If you're certain that you're saved no matter what you do after you accept Christ as Saviour, then you're hardly going to worry about keeping the biblical Sabbath, especially if doing so could cost you your job, home, family, or life.

Another doctrine that anyone leaving Adventism will find among many churches is the idea of a pretribulation rapture. Millions believe that prior to the turmoil preceding the second coming of Jesus, all God's true people will be suddenly, secretly taken to heaven while everyone else remains on earth. Christians will be in their cars, homes, boats, classrooms, wherever—when, instantly, they will quietly disappear, secretly snatched away to be with Jesus in heaven before the tribulation of the last days. Most who hold this idea point to 1 Thessalonians 4:16, 17 in support: "For the Lord himself shall descend from heaven *with a shout, with the voice of the archangel, and with the trump of God:* and the dead in Christ shall rise first: Then we which are alive and remain shall be caught up together with them . . . in the air: and so shall we ever be with the Lord."

Despite the shout, the voice of the archangel, and the trump (trumpet) of God, this verse supposedly teaches that secretly, silently, Christians are going to be taken to heaven while the rest of the world stands around in awe of their sudden disappearance!

What's so dangerous about this doctrine? How could those who believe in the pretribulation rapture be concerned about the mark of the beast and the issues surrounding it if they're certain that the Lord is going to snatch them away before the tribulations and trials of the mark of beast ever come?

Also, almost the whole conservative Christian world expects Christ, *at His return,* to immediately set up His kingdom here on earth, despite what 1 Thessalonians 4:17 says about the saved meeting "the Lord in the air." Most fundamentalists and evangelicals believe that at the second coming Christ will rule on earth for the millennium instead of taking His people to heaven. Writes Tim LaHaye:

One thing that both Jews and Christians agree on is that someday their Messiah is going to come to this earth to set up His Kingdom that shall rule this earth. . . . The millennial kingdom will be a time of faith, when the majority of the population will become believers. . . . Christ will be in charge so there won't be immoral or other forms of destructive TV programming. . . . Body-damaging substances will not be available, so people will not have their minds so fogged that they cannot fairly appraise the truths of Scripture. . . . The university chairs of learning will not be dominated by atheists set to destroy the minds of youth. . . . Even art forms will glorify Christ during the kingdom.[2]

This belief, more than any other, will leave millions of Christians vulnerable to Satan's greatest deception, when he, "as the crowning act in the great drama of deception," fakes Christ's second advent. What better way to be deceived in the last days than by the doctrine that Christ will establish His Kingdom on the earth at His return.

Now the great deceiver will make it appear that Christ has come. In different parts of the earth, Satan will manifest himself among men as a majestic being of dazzling brightness, resembling the description of the Son of God given by John in the Revelation. Revelation 1:13-15. The glory that surrounds him is unsurpassed by anything that mortal eyes have yet beheld. The shout of triumph rings out upon the air: "Christ has come! Christ has come!" The people prostrate themselves in adoration before him, while he lifts up his hands and pronounces a blessing upon them, as Christ blessed His disciples when He was upon the earth.[3]

Another dogma, almost universally accepted among conservative Christians, is that human beings receive immediate reward or punishment at death. Deceived by the idea of an immortal soul, these people believe that the deceased either immediately enter into the presence of Jesus or into the torments of hell. Though many Christians are now somewhat reluctant to envision hell as eternal torment in literal flames, most believe that it involves conscious suffering at some point after death, for eternity.

Again, the point is not to question the salvation, Christian experience, or relationship with Christ of those who believe this; the point is their gross misunderstanding of the nature of man and the character of God. To think that Jesus would allow the lost to suffer for billions and billions and billions of aeons—whether by burning in a literal fire (as many do still believe) or in some other form of conscious torment—is to misunderstand what the Lord is like and the essence of the whole great-controversy scenario. It's hard to fathom how anyone who believes in eternal torment could love God. The theological darkness of this doctrine is almost incomprehensible for those who know the truth about hell.

By not understanding the state of the dead, almost the whole Christian world is susceptible to being duped by spiritualism. How hard it will be for someone, in the confusion of the last days, to accept the seventh-day Sabbath when that person's dearly departed mother returns some night and tells him or her to do otherwise.[4] The deceptions will be overwhelming. Only by being grounded in the truth will anyone be spared from the delusions of the occult.

The above doctrines are some errors that any Adventist seeking fellowship in conservative Christianity would have to deal with. If he seeks out a liberal Christian church, the errors are even worse. Liberal Christianity has all but destroyed true biblical faith. Millions, for example, reject the virgin birth, the deity of Christ, and the divine inspiration of the Bible. Surveys show that a majority of mainline Christian churches aren't even opposed to the concept of evolution as the origin of all species!

Meanwhile, Jehovah's Witnesses teach that "Jesus Christ has returned to earth A.D. 1914."[5] The Mormons believe: "When our Father Adam came into the Garden of Eden, he came into it with a celestial body and brought Eve, *one* of his wives, with him. . . . He is our Father and our God and the only God with whom we have to do."[6] And Christian Science promulgates the tenet that death is "an illusion, for there is no death; the opposite of Good, God, or life. . . . Any material evidence of death is false, for it contradicts the spiritual fact of Being."[7]

No wonder the Lord had to raise up a church with present truth! With doctrines ranging from "once saved, always saved" to Adam being a god, from the pretribulation rapture to eternal torment in hell—

Jesus had to have a corporate body somewhere preaching unsullied doctrine. Otherwise, how could anyone be prepared for the second coming?

---

1. *Testimonies for the Church*, 1:412.

2. Tim LaHaye, *How to Study Bible Prophecy for Yourself* (Eugene, Oreg.: Harvest House, 1990), 159, 168, 169.

3. *The Great Controversy*, 624.

4. See Clifford Goldstein, *Day of the Dragon* (Boise, Idaho: Pacific Press, 1993), 101, 111.

5. Walter Martin, *Kingdom of the Cults* (Grand Rapids, Mich.: Zondervan, 1965), 46.

6. Brigham Young, *The Journal of Discourses*, 1:50. Quoted in Ibid., 178.

7. Mary Baker Eddy, *Science and Health*, 575. Quoted in Ibid., 123.

17

As was true of ancient Israel, God's corporate end-time remnant is distinguished not so much by the errors it avoids, but by the truths it possesses. God's remnant, in whatever age, has had remnant truth, yet this truth has always been taught in the context of "present truth." As time has progressed, the Lord has revealed more light to His remnant. For example, the early Christian church had more truth than did Abraham. Yet these added truths have always rested upon a foundation rooted in antiquity.

The remnant today, for example, keeps the seventh-day Sabbath. But now, along with recognition of the Sabbath as a symbol of the Lord as Creator, Redeemer, and Sanctifier, Adventists know that in the final test of loyalty to God before the second coming, the Sabbath will also constitute the seal of God in contrast to the mark of the beast. The Sabbath remains everything that it has been to the remnant in previous ages, only more. By clinging to the Sabbath, the remnant church—far from coming up with something new—is, like ancient Israel, adhering to light that originated in Eden.

Linked with the Sabbath are the Ten Commandments, long an emphasis of God's remnant. Though most of Christendom pays lip service to the commandments, the violation of the fourth nullifies even that. Meanwhile, the end-time remnant not only keeps the Ten Commandments as a barrier against sin, as have God's faithful through every generation; it understands, as well, the importance of the law in the whole scenario of the great controversy between Christ and Satan.

From the very beginning of the great controversy in heaven it has been Satan's purpose to *overthrow the law of God.* It was to accomplish this that he entered upon his rebellion against the Creator, and though he was cast out of heaven he has continued the same warfare upon the earth. To deceive men, and thus lead them to transgress God's law, is the object which he has steadfastly pursued.... The last great conflict between truth and error is but the final struggle of *the long-standing controversy concerning the law of God.* Upon this battle we are now entering—a battle between the laws of men and the precepts of Jehovah, between the religion of the Bible and the religion of fable and tradition.[1]

In contrast to the myths of its pagan neighbors, the Jews of ancient Israel had the truth about Creation. Adventism enjoys added light in this area too. While millions of Christians accept evolution in one form or another, Adventists still believe that "in six days the Lord made 'the heaven and the earth' and all living things upon the earth, and rested on the seventh day of that first week."[2] Besides the biblical record, the spirit of prophecy (a gift also found in ancient Israel) has given numerous details regarding the Genesis account, which helps explain why the Adventist church still clings to a literal six-day Creation against much of the tide of Protestantism. Belief in the biblical Creation becomes an especially important component of the present-truth message to "worship him that made heaven, and earth, and the sea, and the fountains of waters" (Revelation 14:7). Thus, the Sabbath—meaningful only in the context of the biblical Creation—is seen as the foremost component of worshiping Him who "made heaven, and earth, and the sea" in contrast to those who "worship the beast and his image" (Revelation 14:9).

Like ancient Israel, Adventism also has a sanctuary message. Though other Christian churches understand from the book of Hebrews that a sanctuary in heaven exists (though some, erroneously, see it only as allegory) and that Christ is ministering there in our behalf, Adventism alone understands the present truth of the two-apartment phases of Christ's High Priestly ministry and the pre-advent judgment of the second phase. How interesting, too, that it is after the "time, times, and the dividing of time" in Daniel 7:25 that the pre-advent judgment appears—a unique teaching of the remnant, which also appears after that same "time, and times, and half a time" period (Revelation 12:14).

Adventism's comprehension of the importance and nature of Christ's High Priestly ministry, though advanced light, is rooted in ancient truths that go back to the Israelite sanctuary and temple services as well as the first animal Adam sacrificed after the fall.

Another unique teaching of the remnant today, as in Israel's time, is the health message, although we enjoy greater light than did ancient Israel in this area as well. In an era that highly esteems science, the health message is the only aspect of Adventism that can be verified by science. We can't prove scientifically the state of the dead, the sanctuary message, or the second coming of Christ. But science continually verifies the Adventist message on alcohol, tobacco, vegetarianism, and healthful living in general. Again, like the Hebrews, Adventists are ahead of their neighbors in this area, not because they have developed new, innovative truths, but because we have reached back and grabbed old ones.

Adventism understands the great controversy between Christ and Satan. Most other Christians know little, if anything, about this struggle. Many don't even believe in Satan, and those who do don't begin to have the insights available to Adventists through the Spirit of Prophecy. For example, Ellen White says regarding Satan and his rebellion:

> Satan was once an honored angel in heaven, next to Jesus Christ. His countenance was mild, expressive of happiness like the other angels. His forehead was high and broad, and showed great intelligence. His form was perfect. He had a noble, majestic bearing. . . .
>
> All the angels were astir. Satan was insinuating against the government of God, ambitious to exalt himself, and unwilling to submit to the authority of Jesus. . . .
>
> When Satan became fully conscious that there was no possibility of his being brought again into favor with God, then his malice and hatred began to be manifest. He consulted with his angels, and a plan was laid to still work against God's government. When Adam and Eve were placed in the beautiful garden, Satan was laying plans to destroy them.[3]

The great controversy is an ancient biblical theme, found especially in one of the oldest books, Job. It is not new light that Adventism has on this topic, merely advanced light. More than ever, as this controversy climaxes at the end of the age, the topic becomes present truth.

Finally, and most importantly, like ancient Israel, Adventism enjoys more light on the advent of the Messiah—not just His first advent, which was ancient Israel's specific call, but His second, which is Adventism's special emphasis (though the second becomes meaningful only if taught on the foundation of the first). Israel was to prepare the way for Christ's first advent; Adventism for His second. The name that the church has chosen for itself, Seventh-day *Adventist*, reveals how important the second coming of Christ is to the church's *raison d'être*. This aspect of present truth is even more crucial than most others, especially considering the confusion and numerous misconceptions in Christendom about the second coming. Here again, Adventism has been blessed with truths that set it apart from the rest of the world.

Of course, other churches possess some of these doctrines, but none has Adventism's added insights regarding them. And it's *these truths*, along with others—distinct, clear, biblical, and timed for the present age—that give Adventism its remnant status, just as these and other truths, in their ancient context, did for ancient Israel.

---

1. *The Great Controversy*, 582. Emphasis supplied.
2. *Seventh-day Adventists Believe . . .* , 68.
3. *Spiritual Gifts*, 1:17, 18, 19.

18

Many will argue, however, that the reasoning of the previous chapters is dangerous. *Look at how exclusive ancient Israel became*, they would warn. *Because it saw itself as the remnant, Israel believed that only Israelites would be saved. They thought they alone were the recipients of God's love. They became isolated, exclusive, and wrapped up in their own beliefs and traditions. They thought they were better and holier than anyone else. Because of their exalted calling they treated other faiths with disdain.*

All these charges are correct, but they don't negate one crucial fact: Israel still had the truth! Yes, they accused the Lord of the Sabbath of trampling upon it (see Mark 2:23-28), but at least they had the Sabbath. No doubt, they misused laws about diet and health, but at least they had the laws. Of course, many misinterpreted the prophecies concerning the Messiah, but at least they had the prophecies. No matter how much they misread, misused, and misapplied these truths—they still had more truth than anyone else.

It is the same with Adventism. Even if some Seventh-day Adventists become proud, have a holier-than-thou attitude, or become exclusive because of the church's remnant status or prophetic calling, these problems don't invalidate that status or prophetic calling.

Actually, unlike ancient Israel, this church has never officially taught that its members are the only ones who are saved or that they alone are God's children. Some members might believe these things, but they are on the fringe. The Adventist Church's statement on the remnant itself begins with the broad acknowledgment that true Christians are found in every religious body: "The universal church is composed of all who truly believe in Christ."[1]

Questions on Doctrine aptly expresses the Adventist position:

> We believe that the prophecy of Revelation 12:17 points to the experience and work of the Seventh-day Adventist Church, but we do *not* believe that we *alone* constitute the true children of God—that we are the only true Christians—on earth today. We believe that God has a multitude of earnest, faithful, sincere followers in all Christian communions.[2]

Ellen White believed the same way: "In what religious bodies," she wrote, "are the greater part of the followers of Christ now to be found? *Without doubt*, in the various churches professing the Protestant faith."[3]

Scripture teaches the same principle. Revelation 18 begins with a warning about Babylon, the apostate religio-political system of the last days. "And he cried mightily with a strong voice, saying, Babylon the great is fallen, is fallen, and is become the habitation of devils, and the hold of every foul spirit, and a cage of every unclean and hateful bird" (verse 2). Then, after more condemnation of Babylon, Revelation reads, "And I heard another voice from heaven, saying, Come out of her, *my people*, that ye be not partakers of her sins, and that ye receive not of her plagues" (verse 4). The Lord calls "my people"— His "earnest, faithful, sincere followers in all Christian communions" out of Babylon. Obviously, not all of God's people are now among those who "keep the commandments of God, and have the testimony of Jesus Christ" (Revelation 12:17). Some are still in Babylon.

Also, Scripture distinguishes between the remnant depicted in Revelation 12:17 (undeniably Adventism) and the saints who avoid the mark of the beast prior to the second coming (undeniably a larger group). Amid the warning about the fall of Babylon and the mark of the beast, the faithful are described in these words: "Here is the patience of the saints: here are they that keep the commandments of God, and the faith of Jesus" (Revelation 14:12). Nothing is said about this group having the "testimony of Jesus Christ." That doesn't mean that some of these saints won't have it; many, no doubt, will. It means, instead, that some might not. God's faithful from all religions will one day understand enough regarding the truth to take their stand for Jesus by keeping all His commandments, whether or not they ever have "the testimony of Jesus Christ." What they definitely *will* have, however, is the "*faith* of Jesus." That is the ultimate purpose of the "testimony of Jesus Christ," anyway—to help people acquire the "faith of Jesus." Some, apparently, will acquire the faith of Jesus without the "testimony of Jesus" with which the corporate remnant church has been so blessed.

Also, spiritual exclusiveness and arrogance are hardly the main things against which the Adventist church struggles today. On the contrary, many Adventists don't know what they believe or why they believe it. Thousands no longer recognize the distinctive mission or purpose of the remnant church, much less feel exclusive about it. On the contrary, they are ashamed at the title and even shun it. For them, the only difference between Adventism and other denominations is that Adventists keep the Sabbath and don't eat pork, hardly the stuff prophetic zealots are made of. It's hard enough to boldly claim that your church is the "remnant church" if you really believe it; but if you're having doubts to begin with, you're going to run from that claim. Many already have their Nikes on.

A perfect example of this appeared in a recent video by a former Adventist. In the video, the narrator told about Adventist critic Walter Martin (now deceased) confronting Adventists at a meeting in Loma Linda. Martin denied that the investigative judgment had any scriptural basis and, according to the video, no one answered Martin's charges. This former Adventist was thoroughly bothered by the lack of answers when Walter Martin rejected the investigative judgment.

But who cares? Walter Martin rejected the Sabbath and the truth about the state of the dead as well! Does that invalidate these crucial truths? Of course not! Certainly, we should be concerned when anyone rejects truth, but only because of our care for that person's spiritual well-being—not out of fear that they have rejected it because it isn't truth. Unless, of course, we're harboring doubts about the message ourselves.

As it was, the person narrating this video did have problems with the doctrine. He regurgitated the same tired old arguments against the investigative judgment, arguments that have long been relegated to the trash heap by just about everyone who has seriously—and honestly—studied them. And sure enough, by the time the video ended, this former Adventist openly denied the investigative judgment, which explains why he was so concerned about Walter Martin's rejection of it.

Meanwhile, those who have taken the time to be grounded biblically in the message, don't become too upset or doubtful if someone rejects it; they themselves know what is truth. Almost the entire world will reject our message, so that's hardly a reason to waffle on it now.

The thing that should help make us confident about the message is this: no *doctrinal* alternatives exist. The Lord has made present truth stand out so clearly now, so distinctly, as He has done in every other age, that however hard it might be for someone to become an Adventist, it should be the easiest thing to remain one. What are our other options?

No doubt, the Lord has true followers in every religion. That's not the point. The point is that no other corporate body approaches the present truth that Adventism has. Baptists don't. Jehovah's Witnesses don't. Episcopalians don't. Assemblies of God members don't. Christian Scientists don't. Roman Catholics don't. Methodists, Moonies, and Mormons don't, either. If a seeker for truth can find a church that fits the prophecies concerning the remnant better than Adventism does, a church that not only keeps the commandments, but has "the testimony of Jesus Christ," a church that is preaching the present-truth message of the three angels in Revelation 14 as the last warning message to the world before the second coming of Christ—then that person ought to join such a church.

Good luck.

She'll need it.

---

1. *Seventh-day Adventists Believe . . .* , 152.

2. *Questions on Doctrine*, 187.

3. *The Great Controversy*, 383. Emphasis supplied.

Remnant Within the Remnant

19

If Adventism has all this light, are we holier than those who don't? Does all this "truth" make us better than other Christians? Has the "spirit of prophecy" sanctified us in ways that those without it could never be? Does being the remnant make us more righteous than anyone else?

Most Adventists would answer, "Of course not!"

But why not? With the revelation of Jesus Christ that we possess, Seventh-day Adventists should be the godliest, holiest, and most Christlike people on earth.

Are we?

Please . . . a blindfolded drunk could throw a lasso around members of almost any other church and snare more honest, sincere, loving, and forgiving Christians than exist among Adventists today.

"So Manasseh made Judah and the inhabitants of Jerusalem to err, *and to do worse than the heathen*, whom the Lord had destroyed before the children of Israel" (2 Chronicles 33:9).

Have we not done "worse than the heathen," or at least—the spiritual "Babylonians"?

Revelation 3:15-17 succinctly describes our condition:

> I know thy works, that thou art neither cold nor hot: I would thou wert cold or hot. So then because thou art lukewarm, and neither cold nor hot, I will spue thee out of my mouth. Because thou sayest, I am rich, and increased with goods, and have need of nothing; and knowest not that thou art wretched, and miserable, and poor, and blind, and naked.

Ellen White has repeatedly applied these words, the Laodicean message, to the Seventh-day Adventist Church:

If ever a people were represented by the Laodicean message, it is the people who have had great light, the revelation of the Scriptures, that Seventh-day Adventists have received.[1]

To the church of the present day this message is sent. I call upon our church members to read the whole of the third chapter of Revelation, and to make an application of it. The message to the church of the Laodiceans applies especially to the people of God today.[2]

God is leading out a people. He has chosen people, a church on the earth, whom He has made the depositaries of His law. He has committed to them sacred trust and eternal truth to be given to the world. He would reprove and correct them. The message to the Laodiceans is applicable to Seventh-day Adventists who have had great light and have not walked in the light.[3]

Laodicea lacks holiness, not truth—the problem that has plagued God's corporate remnant in every age.

As a people we are triumphing in the clearness and strength of the truth. We are fully sustained in our positions by an over-whelming amount of plain Scriptural testimony. But we are very much wanting in Bible humility, patience, faith, love, self-denial, watchfulness, and the spirit of sacrifice. We need to cultivate Bible holiness. Sin prevails among the people of God. The plain message of rebuke to the Laodiceans is not received.[4]

The people of God must see their wrongs and arouse to zealous repentance and a putting away of those sins which have brought them into such a deplorable condition of poverty, blindness, wretchedness, and fearful deception. I was shown that the pointed testimony must live in the church. This alone will answer to the message to the Laodiceans. Wrongs must be reproved, sin must be called sin, and iniquity must be met promptly and decidedly, and put away from us as a people.[5]

Her counsels confirm what the Bible has shown explicitly for thousands of years: God's corporate entity has always been a spiritual basket case! When the Lord cried, "I myself will fight against you with an outstretched hand and with a strong arm, even in anger, and in fury, and in great wrath" (Jeremiah 21:5), to whom was He talking? It was to His church! When He warned, "Behold, I will corrupt your seed, and spread dung upon your faces, even the dung of your solemn feasts" (Malachi 2:3), He wasn't warning Amorites, Hittites, Philistines, or Persians, but His corporate remnant! When He said, "The iniquity of the house of Israel and Judah is exceeding great, and the land is full of blood, and the city full of perverseness: for they say, The Lord hath forsaken the earth, and the Lord seeth not" (Ezekiel 9:9), He was referring to His covenant people, those who had been given a revelation of light and truth greater than any other nation around them! All these warning descriptions apply to His corporate remnant church!

Compared to the warnings He poured out upon His remnant centuries ago, our heavenly Father's counsel to His remnant today seems tepid:

> I saw that the remnant were not prepared for what is coming upon the earth. Stupidity, like lethargy, seemed to hang upon the minds of most of those who profess to believe that we are having the last message. My accompanying angel cried out with awful solemnity, "Get ready! get ready! get ready! for the fierce anger of the Lord is soon to come."[6]

> What shall I say to arouse the remnant people of God? I was shown that dreadful scenes are before us; Satan and his angels are bringing all their powers to bear upon God's people. He knows that if they sleep a little longer, he is sure of them, for their destruction is certain.[7]

> There are times when a distinct view is presented to me of the condition of the remnant church, a condition of appalling indifference to the needs of a world perishing for lack of a knowledge

of the truth for this time. . . . Oh, how my heart aches because Christ is put to shame by their un-Christlike behavior![8]

I was shown the low state of God's people; that God had not departed from them; but that they had departed from God, and become lukewarm. They possess the theory of the truth, but lack its saving power. As we near the close of time, Satan comes down with great power knowing his time is short. Especially upon the remnant will his power be exercised.[9]

November 20, 1855, while [I was] in prayer, the Spirit of the Lord suddenly and powerfully came upon me, and I was taken off in vision. I saw that the Spirit of the Lord has been dying away from the church.[10]

As members of God's remnant church, we must pray with firm faith for the gift of the grace of love. Love is the fulfilling of the law, and is manifested altogether too little among those upon whom has been shining great light.[11]

Ellen White is not writing here about Baptists, Methodists, or Anglicans. Her words are for Seventh-day Adventists, whom she describes as in a "low state," a church from whom the Spirit of God was dying away *in the 1850s*, an asleep people with an "appalling indifference" to the needs around them. She said that they have departed from the Lord and, though they have truth, they don't have love—and, without love we are "nothing" (1 Corinthians 13:2). In short, she describes Adventism as Laodicean.

Yet she also depicts Seventh-day Adventists as the remnant church. Can Laodicea be the remnant? Obviously.

Indeed, however pathetic—even "wretched, miserable, poor, blind, and naked"—we are, the Adventist church remains the remnant church, if for no other reason than that it alone possesses the remnant truth. No matter how many child-molesters, libertines, hypocrites, fanatics, or other unconverted degenerates suck the power and spirit out of the body, we are still corporately the remnant because we alone have the remnant truth. And it is ultimately truth, not holiness, that distinguishes God's *corporate* remnant people today just as it did in the days of ancient Israel.

The analogy with ancient Israel works well—to a point. From the making of the golden calf, from the report of the twelve spies, from the split of the nation into two warring factions, from the worldly apostasy of the first temple up through the hard-nosed legalism of the early second temple, Israel remained the remnant nation, God's corporate religious people who alone had "present truth," despite their spiritual weaknesses. Even after the remnant crucified Jesus, the Lord still "confirm[ed] the covenant" (Daniel 9:27) with them for three and a half more years, giving them time as a corporate body to repent of the death of Jesus and accept Him as the Messiah.

Nevertheless, Jesus did finally have to stand over Jerusalem and say, "Behold, your house is left unto you desolate" (Matthew 23:38). He did eventually have to warn the leaders, "Therefore, say I unto you, The kingdom of God shall be taken from you, and given to a nation bringing forth the fruits thereof " (Matthew 21:43). The time came when Israel no longer functioned as a *corporate*, political entity, as *the* remnant church. The Lord had to call out a new people, a new movement, a new church with a new message.

Can the same thing happen to us?

1. *Manuscript Releases*, 18:193.
2. *SDA Bible Commentary*, 7:959.
3. *Selected Messages*, 2:66.
4. *Testimonies for the Church*, 3:253.
5. Ibid., 260.
6. *Early Writings*, 119.
7. *Christian Service*, 81.
8. *Testimonies for the Church*, 8:24.
9. *Spiritual Gifts*, 4B:45.
10. Ibid., 2.
11. *Bible Training School*, 1 June 1903.

20

Anyone who has ever "done Adventism" must have been tempted at some point to question the church's prophetic role. Many, particularly those who have grown up within the system, have seen the crass hypocrisy of those who say and do all the acceptable Adventist things in public while in darkness they commit the vilest sins. Others are turned off by the same platitudes and dogma year after year.

How many of our youth have been frustrated, hurt, even burned by holier-than-thou saints who have judged and condemned them without ever knowing the pain and struggles of their hearts?

How many young people have been raised knowing more about Ellen White than Jesus Christ?

How many have been sickened by the lack of commitment to doctrines and standards?

How many know rules, laws, standards, but not the Lord?

How many have been forced to leave Adventism in order to find the love, assurance, and acceptance that they have craved but never found in the remnant? Years ago, while visiting a charismatic fellowship, I met a young couple who had been raised as Seventh-day Adventists and who had gone through Adventist schools, but who had left the church. The man's brother was even an Adventist minister. During the heat and excitement of the charismatic service, I asked why they had walked out on Adventism.

"When we were in the Adventist church," the husband answered, "our marriage was falling apart. We found here the love and help we needed. Now our marriage is great."

Others, on the contrary, have become concerned about the lowering of standards, the infiltration of liberal theology into our schools, the lack of distinctive Adventism being preached in our pulpits, and the inroads of worldly policy and philosophy in our institutions. Convinced that the church has become Babylon, they have left and joined offshoots. Or they hover on the periphery of the church, diverting tithe, criticizing leadership, dividing churches, and seriously questioning the denomination's prophetic role and remnant status.

What about it? Can the Adventist church lose its remnant status? Can what happened to physical Israel after the death of Christ happen to spiritual Israel today? Will God eventually spit Laodicea *as a whole* out of His mouth and start another body, one that will better fulfill His purposes?

No, because Laodicea is the last church! Revelation chapter 3 ends at verse 22, with the message to the Laodiceans. There is no verse 23 describing another corporate entity. Nothing comes after Laodicea. Blind, wretched, and miserable, we—hard as it is to believe!—are *it*, the last corporate body!

Also, when the Lord called out the Christian church from national Israel, He gave it a distinctive message: Jesus of Nazareth was the Saviour of the world. Not only was that message new light, but it was present truth—new light and present truth that the corporate Jewish nation had missed. This was why the Lord had to form a new church. Had the nation, corporately, accepted the truth, God wouldn't have needed to form a new body. Instead, He had to call out those, both Jews and Gentiles, who would accept and proclaim the message that the corporate Hebrew nation did not accept.

Truth, present truth—not holiness—has been the distinguishing characteristic of God's *corporate* remnant in every age. Thus, as enfeebled and defective as it is, Adventism still has the present-truth message for this time, God's call to men and women everywhere to prepare for Jesus' second coming, the last event prior to the heavenly millennium. No need exists to call out a new church, a remnant with new light or another present-truth message. A new church would have to have a new message, yet what could be more present truth than the second coming?

No doubt, apostasy exists within Adventism, as it always has within God's corporate church. But a church *with* apostasy vastly differs from a church *in* apostasy—and Adventism is not in apostasy, even though apostasy is in it. An apostate church wouldn't have published *Seventh-day Adventists Believe . . . : A Biblical Exposition of 27 Fundamental Doctrines*. Nor would it have published the seven volumes of the Daniel and Revelation Committee Series, all written to defend basic Adventist doctrine. A church spreading all over the world the truth about Jesus, salvation, the Sabbath, the state of the dead, the second coming, and the sanctuary is not in apostasy. An apostate church wouldn't be daily presenting these great truths to thousands in almost every nation. And an apostate church would not print and sell each year hundreds of thousands of books such as *The Great Controversy*, *The Desire of Ages*, *Steps to Christ*, *Education*, *The Ministry of Healing*, and *Patriarchs and Prophets*.

The Adventist church has its Judases, Ahabs, and Jezebels. We probably have more than many members realize. Who could deny that we are not what we should be? We're probably even worse than we think; after all, that's Laodicea's big problem. And how sad that some aren't teaching our truths with the conviction, clarity, and faith that they should. But even watered-down, the three angels' messages are closer to present truth than what many other churches are teaching. No matter how bad the church supposedly is, the Lord is still using it—and it alone—to bring this special message to the world. It wasn't Baptists, charismatics, Presbyterians, or Episcopalians who first taught me the three angels' messages of Revelation 14. I learned them only from Seventh-day Adventists, the only people anyone else is ever going to learn them from as well! Ellen White says,

> Although there are evils existing in the church, and will be until the end of the world, the church in these last days is to be the light of the world that is polluted and demoralized by sin. The church, enfeebled and defective, needing to be reproved, warned, and counseled, is the only object upon earth upon which Christ bestows His supreme regard."[1]

Nevertheless many Adventists are concerned about trends in the church, and justifiably so. Not only have standards been lowered, our distinctive message is not often heard anymore. We're as unlikely to hear a sermon about the investigative judgment as we are about the second coming, victory over sin, or any other unique aspect of present truth. In their desire to preach good "gospel" sermons, some ministers are so imbalanced on their presentation of justification by faith and assurance of salvation that their gospel is not good, for the true gospel is more than justification.

Thus, many members long for the old days, when the church was preaching the "old message," undiluted and unencumbered with such things as justification by faith, grace, and the assurance of salvation. They long for the time when minsters stood in the pulpits and breathed fire about the ongoing investigative judgment and how we had better be absolutely sinless and perfect or our names are going to be blotted out of the book of life, damning us to eternal destruction in the lake of fire awaiting those who rise in the second resurrection. For them, the great days of Adventism were when many congregations wouldn't let jewelry, rock music, or "negroes" in their doors.

In reality, no "good old days" ever existed. Adventism has never had only pure ministers preaching pure truth to pure saints. As far back as 1888, some conservative leaders rejected a powerful message of justification by faith. All the counsel, warning, and rebukes from Sister White about worldliness, lukewarmness, apostasy, fanaticism, racism, immorality, adultery, selfishness, corruption, unsanctified ministers, jealousy, legalism, gossip, masturbation, wayward youths, stealing of tithe, spouse abuse, rebellion, rejection of the testimonies, and other problems lurid enough to make Hollywood blush, were written to the remnant church *in her time*, supposedly the good old days when this church was standing for the truth. How often did she weep for the church—back then! Yet the Lord didn't reject His corporate body then, and He isn't going to reject it now.

Nevertheless, there is a growing movement today away from the denomination—a movement toward a church within a church, or even separation. Factions are already ordaining their own ministers and starting their own churches. Unless these groups and the remnant church can end the rifts, a split will occur. Such a schism would be tragic for these movements because they would be going directly against Spirit of Prophecy counsel (and quite ironic because one of their gripes about the church is that *it* is going against the Spirit of Prophecy). A separation would hurt the denomination too; it can be helped and strengthened by what many of these people have to offer.

Many disgruntled Adventists already believe that the church is in apostasy and that the Lord will call out from it a faithful remnant as He did with the early Christian church. Those involved with the more radical movements believe that they are the faithful ones, the true remnant, and that the Lord is now calling them away from the organized Seventh-day Adventist denomination. Some even believe that the organized Adventist church will eventually link up with the state to persecute the faithful. Many who at one point would have recoiled at the thought of ever leaving the denomination and joining another group have done just that. Others will follow despite Ellen White's warning that

> the church may appear as [if it is] about to fall, but it does not fall. It remains, *while the sinners in Zion will be sifted out*—the chaff separated from the precious wheat. This is a terrible ordeal, but nevertheless it must take place.[2]

Separationists explain away this reference by their definition of "the church," which, according to them, is composed only of faithful people. "It is becoming popular to define the church as consisting of only faithful souls. In connection with this is the thought that the visible Seventh-day Adventist Church, composed of both good and evil influences, is not really God's church at all."[3] Yet Ellen White's quote itself proves that "the church" cannot be just "faithful souls"; otherwise, how could "the sinners in Zion" be sifted out? The reference itself defines the church as having sinners in it—not just faithful souls—and it is these sinners in Zion, not the saints, who are sifted out and leave.

Never did Ellen White hint that because of apostasy the Lord would call out a new people. She warned that apostasy would keep us here longer than we should be, but she never countenanced joining new organizations. On the contrary, she warned:

> Every truth that He [God] has given for these last days is to be proclaimed to the world. Every pillar that He has established is to be strengthened. We cannot now step off the foundation that God has established. We cannot now enter into any new organization; for this would mean apostasy from the truth.[4]

No advice or sanction is given in the Word of God to those

who believe the third angel's message to lead them to suppose that they can draw apart. This you may settle with yourselves forever. It is the devising of unsanctified minds that would encourage a state of disunion.[5]

The concept that the Lord is going to call out a new movement runs into another major flaw. When is the calling-out process going to be complete? If a new movement were to be called out of Adventism, how long would it be before that movement, in turn, would fall into some of the same sins that its founders now accuse the denomination of having fallen into? How long before some members in the new movement decide that *it* is now in apostasy and form another one? And how long before those in even that movement feel called to start a new one?

Sooner or later the Lord has to have His final corporate body. He does. The book of Revelation, chapter 3, shows who.

It's called—Laodicea.

---

1. *Testimonies to Ministers*, 49.
2. *Selected Messages*, 2:380, emphasis supplied.
3. Ty Gibson and James Rafferty, *Trials and Triumph of the Remnant Church* (Malo, Wash.: Light Bearers, 1992), 17, 18.
4. *Selected Messages*, 2:390. Emphasis supplied.
5. Ibid., 3:21.

21

During the patriarchal age, the remnant consisted of only a family of (sometimes) faithful followers of the Lord. The remnant was not an official, corporate body, but rather a family who chose to enter into a covenant relationship with God. Since then, the Lord has had His corporate remnant, an "official," visible people to whom He has given the greatest light regarding Himself and His specific truths for that time. Yet God has also had His spiritual people, the remnant *within* the remnant, those within that corporate body who are actually saved by that truth. A big difference exists between the two.

This contrast appears in Revelation in the message to Thyatira, one of the seven of the Lord's churches. Though judgment is announced against Thyatira for apostasy, the Lord mentions a faithful remnant within it:

> But to the rest [*rest* is the same word for "remnant" found in Revelation 12:17] of you in Thyatira, who do not hold this [false] teaching, who have not learned what some call the deep things of Satan, to you I say, I do not lay upon you any other burden; only hold fast what you have, until I come (Revelation 2:24, 25, RSV).

In Thyatira, the Lord distinguished among those who were faithful, in contrast to the larger body, which wasn't. That's the way it has generally been since Sinai. Membership in the corporate remnant no more guarantees salvation than membership in a health club guarantees good health. Ancient Israel had been God's corporate remnant

107

for more than a thousand years, but not every Israelite was saved. Not everyone in Thyatira was saved either. Will it be any different with Adventism?

Of course not. Many Adventists don't even know what the truth is, much less are they saved by it. If many Adventists barely follow Christ now, what will they do when they face the wrath of the beast and his image? "If thou hast run with the footmen, and they have wearied thee, then how canst thou contend with horses? and if in the land of peace, wherein thou trustedst, they wearied thee, then how wilt thou do in the swelling of Jordan?" (Jeremiah 12:5). When the trouble starts, people will leave the church so quickly that there will be nothing but faint clouds of dust where there were once Seventh-day Adventists.

> As the storm approaches, a large class who have professed faith in the third angel's message, but have not been sanctified through obedience to the truth, *abandon their position and join the ranks of the opposition.*[1]

> Soon God's people will be tested by fiery trials, and the great proportion of those who now appear to be genuine and true will prove to be base metal. Instead of being strengthened and confirmed by opposition, threats, and abuse, they will cowardly *take the side of the opposers.*[2]

> The time is not far distant when the test will come to every soul. The mark of the beast will be urged upon us. Those who have step by step yielded to worldly demands and conformed to worldly customs will not find it a hard matter to yield to the powers that be, rather than subject themselves to derision, insult, threatened imprisonment, and death. The contest is between the commandments of God and the commandments of men. In this time the gold will be separated from the dross in the church.[3]

> There will be a shaking of the sieve. The chaff must be separated from the wheat. Because iniquity abounds, the love of many waxes cold. It is the very time when the genuine will be the strongest. There will be a separation from us of those who have not appreciated the light nor walked in it.[4]

These references, and the one about sinners in Zion being "sifted out," teach three points:

• A separation will occur between the faithful and the unfaithful within the remnant church.

• This separation happens in relation to the mark of the beast and the persecution of the last days.

• Those who prove unfaithful will *leave the church* and join with the opposition.

That last point is crucial. Some critics of the church use the analogy of the Lord calling the Protestant reformers out of Rome, or the early church out of Israel, as examples of what the Lord will do in calling a faithful people out of Adventism as the corporate church itself becomes their persecutors. Interestingly enough, "Laodicea" means "a people judged," and it's often in the context of judgment that the idea of a remnant is found in Scripture. Yet if Laodicea is the last church, as the Bible teaches it is, and if there will be a separation between the wheat and the chaff in the church, as we are told there will be, and if the sinners in Zion will be "sifted out," as Ellen White clearly states—then the division will occur only as the unfaithful leave the church. How could it happen any other way? It will not come as a result of a faithful group withdrawing from an apostate church.

Remember, this separation happens during the persecution of the last days, not before. Though the church has been going through a shaking since Ellen White's day, the real test of faithfulness to Jesus comes when the mark of the beast will be urged upon the church at *the end of the world,* just before Christ returns. Jesus stated that the wheat and the tares grow together "until the harvest: and in the time of harvest I will say to the reapers, Gather ye together first the tares, and bind them in bundles to burn them: but gather the wheat into my barn" (Matthew 13:30). At this time, the wheat and the tares, not just in Adventism, but everywhere, will be separated. The difference is that the wheat in other churches will join with those who already "keep the commandments of God, and have the testimony of Jesus" (Revelation 12:17), while the unfaithful within Adventism will "abandon their position, and join the ranks of the opposers."

No question, a separation will occur within us. Too much sin, coldness, selfishness, and evil exists for the Lord to take the corporate body through to the kingdom as it now stands. And who knows if a corporate, organized Seventh-day Adventist church body will even exist at the end. Ultimately, the faithful will either be in jail, dead, or in hiding. It hardly sounds as if the organization is going to remain as it now is.

Until then, how nice if the dross could be turned into gold by some spiritual alchemy, or the tares become wheat through some cross-breeding process. Unfortunately, that's not how it will be for most. Instead, facing persecution, "a large class who have professed faith in the three angels' messages, but have not been sanctified by obedience to the truth," will not only leave, but turn against us.

What distinguishes the two groups? If those who leave were not "sanctified by the truth," then those who stay must have been. These are the ones who don't merely *know* the truth but *live* it, who don't just know *about Jesus* but who *know Jesus*, who through their personal relationship with Him love the Lord and want to have Christ "formed" in them (Galatians 4:19). They are a modern version of those in every age of the church who have remained true to the Lord even when the masses weren't. They are a remnant *within* the remnant.

> Woe to her that is filthy and polluted, to the oppressing city! She obeyed not the voice; she received not correction; she trusted not in the Lord; she drew not near to her God. . . . I will also leave in the midst of thee an afflicted and poor people, and they shall trust in the name of the Lord. *The remnant of Israel shall not do iniquity, nor speak lies; neither shall a deceitful tongue be found in their mouth* (Zephaniah 3:1, 2, 12, 13, emphasis supplied).

> While a large number of professing believers would deny their faith by their works, there would be a remnant who would endure to the end.[5]

As in Elijah's time, when the Lord had preserved "seven thousand in Israel, all the knees which have not bowed unto Baal, and every mouth which hath not kissed him" (1 Kings 19:18), the Lord has His faithful in spiritual Israel today. Yet just as Elijah didn't know who those individuals were, we don't either. Who really knows what is in people's hearts? How can we understand their deepest struggles? Who knows the abuse and suffering their malleable souls faced as children? Who can see the kinks in their genes? Therefore, we have been admonished not to judge. "Judge not, that ye be not judged. For with what judgment ye judge, ye shall be judged: and with what measure ye mete, it shall be measured to you again" (Matthew 7:1-3). How often the things we're so quick to accuse in others, we ourselves are guilty of as well. "Therefore thou art inexcusable, O man, whosoever thou art that judgest: for wherein thou judgest another, thou condemnest thyself; for thou that judgest doest the same things" (Romans 2:1).

When Jesus was in the flesh, He spent much more time ministering to sinners *in the church* than condemning them. Shouldn't we do the same? Yet it's more in vogue today to criticize the church rather than to pray for it. It's more fun to gossip about the sins of the saints than to sacrifice our time and energy to remedy them. It's easier to be "an accuser of our brethren" (Revelation 12:10) than it is to "sigh and . . . cry for all the abominations" (Ezekiel 9:4) done in the land.

No doubt, the church is not what it should be. It never has been, not now, nor one hundred years ago, nor twenty-five hundred years ago. Thus, those who feel its their calling to find fault with the church will never be out of a job because there's plenty of dirt to go around.

Those, however, who feel that their calling is to be like Jesus will never be out of work, either. Enough hurting, suffering saints exist to keep busy those who want to minster to them as Jesus did. How often we want to preach a powerful sermon for Jesus that will get the congregation trembling before the Lord, or teach a Sabbath School class that will draw big crowds, or donate lots of money for a major mission project. Yet at the same time we have all around us, not only in the community, but in the church, souls who need ministering to just as badly as those whom Christ helped in the remnant church two thousand years ago. Our words, our kindness, our self-sacrificing love in behalf of others in the church could make the difference in whether these erring, weak ones will take their stand for Jesus when the test comes. Criticizing, condemnation, and gossip will surely help push them into the enemy's camp—and will help drag us there too.

No doubt, a fearful, painful shaking of the remnant church will come. The wheat and the tares will be separated. But it's a process that the Lord does, not us. Our job is to love Jesus and those for whom He died, both within and without the church, to help prepare them and ourselves for the great day of the Lord, when He shall preserve a remnant from within the remnant.

> The day of the Lord cometh, for it is nigh at hand; a day of darkness and of gloominess, a day of clouds and of thick darkness, . . . And it shall come to pass, that whosoever shall call on the name of the Lord shall be delivered: for in mount Zion and in Jerusalem shall be deliverance, as the Lord hath said, and in the remnant whom the Lord shall call (Joel 2:1, 2, 32).

---

1. *The Great Controversy*, 608. Emphasis supplied.
2. *Testimonies for the Church*, 5:136. Emphasis supplied.
3. Ibid., 81.
4. Letter 46, 1887, 6.
5. *Adventist Review*, 26 September 1912.

The Abandonment

22

From the beginning of His earthly sojourn, Jesus was possessed of one purpose: He lived to bless others. From His earliest days in Galilee, until He gasped His final breaths on the cross, Christ's life of self-denial and self-sacrifice was all for the good of humanity. His compassion knew no bounds; His ministry no limits. If there were the sick, He healed them; if there were the depressed, he cheered them; if there were the hopeless, He brought them hope. No pain was too small, no person too insignificant, no cry too faint for Jesus. How often he turned weeping into laughing, shouts of agony into shouts of praise, tears of sadness into tears of joy. From city to city, village to village, home to home, Jesus worked tirelessly, preaching the gospel and healing the sick—the King of the universe garbed in humanity.

Through Him, those blind from birth had their eyes filled with light; those hobbling on crippled limbs ran free like deer; those rotting in death awoke in the vigor of youth. All because of—and *only* because of—Jesus. Every word He spoke, every deed He did, was all for the uplifting of humanity.

What more could heaven have given than it gave in the Saviour? "What could have been done more to my vineyard, that I have not done in it?" (Isaiah 5:4). He came, He ministered, He healed, He forgave, He comforted, He taught—He poured out all that God Himself could as a man.

Yet, what happened?

After these things Jesus went over the sea of Galilee, which is the sea of Tiberias. And a great multitude followed him, because they saw his miracles which he did on them that were diseased. And Jesus went up into a mountain, and there he sat with his disciples (John 6:1-3).

Ministry had exhausted Jesus, and He needed a rest. So with the twelve He went to a secluded place. But the people followed anyway, bringing their sickness, pains, and suffering with them for the Master to heal, comfort, and soothe with a stroke, with a word, with a touch. Soon "Jesus . . . lifted up his eyes, and saw a great company come unto him" (John 6:5), and, having compassion on them, He wanted to feed His flock.

"There is a lad here," said Andrew, "which hath five barley loaves, and two small fishes: but what are they among so many?" (John 6:9).

Five loaves, two fish, among "five thousand" (verse 10)? Each one might get a bone and a few crumbs. Yet Jesus sat the people down in groups and multiplied the fish and the bread until men, women, and children "were filled" (verse 12), and enough remained to load twelve baskets.

How did the crowd respond? Ellen White writes:

All day the conviction has strengthened. That crowning act [the feeding of the five thousand] is assurance that the long-looked-for Deliverer is among them. The hopes of the people rise higher and higher. This is He who will make Judea an earthly paradise, a land flowing with milk and honey. He can satisfy every desire. He can break the power of the hated Romans. He can deliver Judah and Jerusalem. He can heal the soldiers who are wounded in battle. He can supply whole armies with food. He can conquer the nations, and give to Israel the long-sought dominion.[1]

And so what did the multitude want to do?

"Jesus therefore perceived that they would come and take him by force, *to make him a king*" (John 6:15, emphasis supplied). So impressed were the masses by this miracle, so amazed at the potential they saw in Him, that they wanted to crown Him king, the long-sought-for Deliverer of Israel. Here is the One through whom the nation would reach the pinnacle of majesty they believed was their due. They set their worldly hopes upon Jesus. He was going to satisfy their dreams of power and glory.

But how does the verse end?

"When Jesus therefore perceived that they would come and take him by force, to make him a king, *he departed again into a mountain himself alone*" (John 6:15, emphasis supplied).

What? Jesus thwarted their plans? He would not allow them to crown Him king? He would not fulfill their expectations after all?

The people didn't like that, not at all. They had set their worldly hopes upon Him, and Jesus disappointed them, badly.

> When Christ forbade the people to declare Him king, He knew that a turning point in His history was reached. Multitudes who desired to exalt Him to the throne today would turn from Him tomorrow. The disappointment of their selfish ambition would turn their love to hatred, and their praise to curses.[2]

The next day, in a synagogue in Capernaum, Jesus said, "I am that bread of life. Your fathers did eat manna in the wilderness, and are dead. . . . I am the living bread which came down from heaven: if any man eat of this bread, he shall live for ever: and the bread that I will give is my flesh, which I will give for the life of the world" (John 6:48-51). The essence of His sermon was that the people needed to partake of His nature and conform to His character. If they wanted to be His followers, "it required the complete surrender of themselves to Jesus. They were called to become self-sacrificing, meek and lowly in heart. They must walk in the narrow path traveled by the Man of Calvary, if they would share in the gift of life and the glory of heaven."[3]

As a result of His words and His failure the day earlier to be crowned king, "many of His disciples went back, and walked no more with him" (John 6:66).

The multitudes, who had been so enthusiastic about Jesus, who had benefited so much from His divine power, who were so grateful for what He had done that they wanted to make Him king—now abandoned Him instead. And, if that were not bad enough, many turned against Him as well. "They sustained their course by gathering up every item that could be turned against Him; and such indignation was stirred up by these false reports that His life was in danger."[4]

Of course, this crisis in Galilee wasn't the last time that Jesus faced a similar situation. When He rode into Jerusalem during the last days of His ministry, some in the crowd who shouted, "Hosanna to the son of David: Blessed is he that cometh in the name of the Lord; Hosanna in the highest" (Matthew 21:9), shouted, "Crucify him" (Mark 15:13) only a few days later!

After the Capernaum sermon, when so many turned away, Jesus looked to the twelve, those who had been closest to Him, those with whom He had shared the greatest truths, those who knew the most about His ministry, and asked, "Will ye also go away?" (John 6:67).

"Then Simon Peter answered him, Lord, to whom shall we go? thou hast the words of eternal life. And we believe and are sure that thou are that Christ, the Son of the living God" (John 6:68, 69).

Yet, what happened?

Judas, of course, not only abandoned Jesus, but betrayed Him, trading thirty pieces of silver for the life of the Son of God. Judas had loved Jesus and had been moved and convicted by the Saviour's life and ministry, yet under the right set of circumstances, he betrayed his Master.

What about the eleven?

Matthew, describing the arrest of Jesus in Gethsemene, wrote, "Then all the disciples forsook him, and fled" (Matthew 26:56). Mark, recounting the same event, wrote: "And they all forsook him, and fled" (Mark 14:50). Even brash Peter not only forsook Him, but before the night was over he denied three times having anything to do with Jesus.

For different reasons, under different circumstances, everyone associated with Jesus abandoned Him and ran. Some, of course, came back, but in His most trying hour Jesus was alone. The rulers hated Him. The mob was against Him. Judas betrayed Him. The disciples forsook Him. Peter denied Him. Jesus was forced to go it alone, A-L-O-N-E!

Now, what does the abandonment of Jesus have to do with us, the corporate remnant church?

For years, Adventists have anticipated the shaking time, the final separation of the wheat and the tares, when many, under the threat of persecution, will "abandon their position and join the ranks of the opposers."[5] The scenario has been told over and over again in books, articles, and sermons: families will be broken up, parents will rise up against children, children against parents, friends against friends, and church members against church members.

Though we all have notions about what this shaking will be like, many Adventists really have no idea what will be the devil's most ingenious ploy to separate us from the truth. We will be undermined and shaken in ways that we don't dare anticipate, by methods that the Sabbath School quarterly will never tell you about.

Sometimes I get glimpses, little bursts of insight, as to what the devil will do to us—and I shudder, not just for myself, but for the church. I think: *Our people aren't ready for this!* When I anticipate these unexpected assaults, and then look out upon a lukewarm, Laodicean people numbed by the world, one image burns across my mind: *sheep going to the slaughter*.

Strong words, but as a church we will be attacked from angles we don't expect and thus are not prepared for. Everything that can be shaken will, indeed, be shaken—and in ways we have never planned upon.

A remedy exists, however, to help prepare ourselves. We must be able, through the grace of God, to withstand one of Satan's nastiest means of severing people from Jesus and His truth for this time. I have been gearing myself up for years, because I've seen it coming for years.

What is the answer?

We need to separate—totally, 100 percent, *no exceptions*—our faith, our love of Jesus, our love of the truth, from everybody and every-thing, including, even especially!, *the Seventh-day Adventist Church*.

I'm not talking about leaving the denomination. Please! There's no little hypocrisy in those who separate from the body because it isn't following the counsels, when some of the clearest counsel tells us not to leave. By the grace of God, the only way I'd leave the Adventist church is if I were thrown out—and I would still send it my tithe! If the Adventist church sent my tithe money to Saddam Hussein, I'd continue to be a Seventh-day Adventist.

What, then, do I mean about completely separating our faith from the church?

Suppose, after you finish reading this book, you hear that Clifford Goldstein has left Adventism because he was caught running a drug-dealing operation out of his office at the General Conference.

How would you feel? Bad (I would hope). But is Christ's death nullified because Goldstein turned out to be a criminal? Does the Sabbath change to Sunday because Goldstein was a hypocrite? Is Christ's High Priestly ministry no longer valid because all the time Goldstein was writing and preaching he was also dealing drugs?

Of course not.

Suppose the person who worked so hard to win you to Jesus, who studied with you, who wept with you, who prayed with you, who is responsible for your knowing Jesus—suppose you found out that all along this person was molesting children?

Is righteousness by faith made void, even if a child molester first taught it to you? Is Ellen White's prophetic gift nullified even if a pederast were the one to first introduce you to those books? Does the message become false even if the person who brought it to you lusted after your five-year-old?

Of course not.

Suppose a church leader, one whom you respected, who fed your soul, whose words, demeanor, or example sparked a spiritual light inside you—suppose all along he was a practicing homosexual?

Does present truth change as a result? Do we no longer have to obey the Ten Commandments? Is Adventism no longer the corporate remnant? Are the dead suddenly in heaven or hell?

Of course not.

No matter what anyone, anywhere, in the church does, no matter how much apostasy, corruption, scandal, and sin exists in the church—the truth remains the truth. No one in this church can do anything to nullify, or even alter, one aspect of the three angels' messages any more than a conference-committee decision could alter the sun in its course.

Yet, the crucial question is: Are you grounded enough in Jesus, are you confident enough of this message, that if the people you love and admire the most were to turn out to be some of the most vile, unrepentant Judases since Judas himself, you would remain firm? Are you sure enough of the truth that you would not leave it—no matter what anyone, anywhere, in the church did, said, or became?

How many people have been lost because they had their eyes on sinful, erring human beings and not on the only sinless unerring Human that ever lived? For this reason, we need to separate our faith from anyone and anything, even and especially those in the church, and center it only on Jesus.

Of course, we can get help from others in the church when we need it. We can lean on others in times of hurt. We need to love each other, to bear one another's burdens, to be willing to lay down our lives for each other. We need so desperately to be the caring, loving church body that Jesus wants us to be and that we're not. But, in the end, when push comes to shove, when the day of testing will hit every soul, we need to be able to stand alone, trusting in the Lord and His Word and in no one else, because no one else can be entirely trusted.

Perhaps you are in the Adventist church today because somebody loved you into the message. Perhaps the only reason you are here is because some Adventist or Adventists revealed to you the love and character of Jesus by the life they lived. Perhaps you are a member of a loving, caring, Christ-centered Adventist church where you enjoy the fellowship and support of the saints. Even so, you need an experience with Jesus that will go beyond the fellowship and love you find at potlucks and church picnics. You need an experience that will remain fastened to Jesus and this truth regardless of what others in the church might do. However much a loving Christian may have had to do with bringing you to Jesus and the church—if that's the only reason you remain in the church, then sooner or later the devil will make sure you meet a nasty, unsanctified Adventist who will drive you out a lot faster than you were loved in.

Be warned: The shaking of Adventism isn't going to be as clear-cut as we envision. If it were going to be just the big, bad, mean, old pork-eating, Sunday-keeping Catholics and apostate Protestants picking on us nice, sweet, holy, Vege-Link-eating Seventh-day Adventists because of the Sabbath/Sunday issue, surviving the shaking would be relatively easy. Yet it's not going to be that simple. It's one thing if other Adventists—even ministers and leaders—are thrown in jail because they refuse to compromise on the Sabbath. What inspiration and strength we would draw from their faithfulness! But what will we do when people we look up to are thrown in jail *because that's where they have belonged all along?* How much easier it would be if the world hates us because we're standing firm for truth while it is condemned and convicted of rejecting the law of God. But who is ready for the time, perhaps at the beginning of the final crisis, when the world hates us, not because we are holy and righteous, but *because we deserve to be hated?*

Jesus said that an "enemy came and sowed tares among the wheat" (Matthew 13:25), and the enemy has sown his tares within Adventism. Wouldn't it make sense for him to try to bring more tares into the remnant church, the people with present truth? And would it not be one of the devil's great ploys to wait until the right moment before he exposes these tares to the world in a way that will severely embarrass, even shake the faith of, others? And what better time would that be than just before, or even during, the Sunday-law crisis?

Waco should awaken us to the devil's plans. Though the church had long ago disfellowshiped David Koresh, who among us didn't feel embarrassed, even apologetic, about being a Seventh-day Adventist while Waco was splashed across the evening news? Now, suppose that Sunday-law agitation had started in the first few weeks after Koresh and his band of deluded followers killed federal police. Imagine how much harder it would be to present the law of God while this aberrant group with ties to Seventh-day Adventists was holed up at Ranch Apocalypse shooting at the ATF agents! How much harder it would be to teach the three angels' messages of Revelation 13 while Koresh was rambling on about the seven seals of Revelation!

Ellen White warned that "the work which the church has failed to do in a time of peace and prosperity she will have to do in a terrible crisis under most discouraging, forbidding circumstances,"[6] but who would expect circumstances this forbidding and discouraging? Even worse, what if those who will shame us aren't Branch Davidians, but Seventh-day Adventists?

If we thought Waco was bad . . . just wait.

"For there is nothing covered," Jesus said, "that shall not be revealed; neither hid, that shall not be known" (Luke 12:2). Who can imagine what's covered and hidden among us? And who wants to be there when it's all revealed and made known?

Therefore, our only defense against this particular assault —when that which is covered is revealed, and that which is hidden is made known—must be a deep settling into the truth, both intellectually and experientially. We must have a faith that transcends the church and everyone in it, a faith that leans only upon the Lord. A faith like Jesus had.

Perhaps, for this reason, God's final remnant are described as those who not only keep the commandments of God, but who have "the faith of Jesus" (Revelation 14:12). Though we often use this text to identify ourselves, such a use is not quite correct. Unlike the remnant in Revelation 12:17, which appears sometime after the 1,260-year period and, no doubt, refers to the corporate remnant church, the saints in Revelation 14:12 appear only in the conflict regarding the beast and his image—a still-future struggle. These are a people who are not yet revealed.

Whoever they ultimately are (the text doesn't say Seventh-day Adventists, though let's hope there'll be some among them), two specific characteristics identify these people: (1) they keep the commandments of God, and (2) they have the faith of Jesus. Their remnant position is built upon two tiers. One is doctrinal, because they know that God requires them to keep His commandments; and one is experiential, because they have a faith experience with God as Jesus had.

On the first tier, these people are firmly rooted in the Word. They know what they believe and why they believe it. They are not counting on their pastor, church leaders, or the ways of the world to guide them. They themselves, firmly grounded in the Word of God, know what the Lord asks of them and, despite economic and political pressure, they will keep God's commandments because they know, intellectually, from His Word, that obedience to His law is what the Lord commands.

The second tier is based on their experience. The "faith of Jesus," no doubt, encompasses many things, but the last days of Christ's life show that it includes a faith that will stand alone and that will endure to the end—the faith of the remnant.

Indeed, Jesus was the true remnant, a symbol not of those who merely know truth, but of those who in the end are actually saved by it. Some Hebrew words used for *remnant* mean "to remain," "to be left over," and at the end of Jesus' earthly life and ministry, He was the only one remaining, the only one left of His core band of followers, the nucleus through whom He would form the new Israel. He alone remained faithful, while those around Him scattered and fled during a time of persecution. Thus, he was, in a real sense, "the remnant of the remnant."

In these last days, those who seek to be among "the remnant of the remnant" will need the "faith of Jesus." One of the clearest aspects of Christ's faith was that it remained firm though everyone around Him apostatized, fled, rejected, or persecuted Him. Though He craved human support, comfort, and encouragement, it was His faith that enabled Him not to rely on these things.

In Gethsemene, for example, how much Jesus could have used the prayers and encouragement of His most trusted disciples. Instead, three times He found them sleeping. Yet His faith enabled Him to rise above Judas's betrayal, Peter's denial, and the disciples fleeing. It was a faith that—pained by taunts, injured by jeers, hurt by hatred, stung by rejection—nevertheless wasn't shaken because of any of them. Jesus' faith did not depend upon humanity. It was totally between Him and the Father, as our faith also needs to be. As the world was against Jesus, so it will be against us. And not only will the world oppose us; many who have been closest to us will abandon us, turn against us, and perhaps— most painfully—disappoint and embarrass us.

We need to reach out for the "substance of things hoped for, the evidence of things not seen" (Hebrews 11:1) because the things seen can, and almost inevitably will, disappoint us. We need, like Jesus, not to look to the earthly, the temporal, but to the heavenly and the eternal, especially because sooner or later the earthly, the temporal, will turn around and bite us. Heaven never will.

Fortunately, time remains to acquire "the faith of Jesus." This major characteristic of the remnant of the remnant is the only one that matters. Being in the corporate remnant won't save you any more than it did Ahab, Absalom, or Judas. Adventism doesn't guarantee that you'll be among the final, faithful remnant, which will be composed of those—whatever their background—who come to a saving relationship with Jesus Christ that is manifested in obedience to "the commandments of God." As Adventists, we have great opportunities to be a part of that group—much greater than those of other backgrounds— but unless we take advantage of these opportunities, our condemnation will be worse than anyone else's because, as Jesus said, "Unto whomsoever much is given, of him shall be much required" (Luke 12:48).

Thus, what Adventists need is an experience with the Lord that will enable them to survive, as Jesus did, the shaking from within as well as the pressure from without. And the only way they're going to get such an experience is the way Jesus did, through a life of communion, prayer, and obedience to the Father.

For starters, Adventists need to spend less time watching television and more time reading the Bible; less time talking to each other and more time talking to God; less time thinking about what we can do for ourselves and more time thinking about what we can do for the Lord; less time seeking to know the ways of the world and more time seeking to know Jesus. Only those who know Him well enough to be willing to die for Him are going to stand as part of that final faithful group.

> Seek ye the Lord while he may be found, call ye upon him while he is near: Let the wicked forsake his way, and the unrighteous man his thoughts: and let him return unto the Lord, and he will have mercy upon him; and to our God, for he will abundantly pardon (Isaiah 55:6, 7).

Those words were for God's corporate remnant back then, just as they are for it today. The Lord wants to "have mercy" upon the wicked and to "abundantly pardon" the unrighteous. Who can deny the wickedness and unrighteousness among Seventh-day Adventism? You don't need to look beyond the person in the pew next to you to find it— or even that far. Look within. Nevertheless, "God commendeth his love toward us, in that, while we were yet sinners, Christ died for us" (Romans 5:8). That includes the tares within the Adventist church.

The Lord has made a way to forgive that remnant-church father who molested his daughter, that old lady who hurled a judgmental look upon a woman wearing pearls, that Pathfinder leader who beat his wife, that church member who opened his motorcycle dealership on Sabbath, and even that Adventist physician who murdered a man in his office.

Christ died not only for these people, but for those damaged by their sin, for the twelve-year-old molested girl, for the woman in pearls, for the battered spouse of the wifebeater, for the children of the divorced parents, for any person ever hurt, frustrated, and embittered by Seventh-day Adventists. Nothing ever happened to them that Jesus doesn't know about, that He doesn't care about, that He doesn't want to heal.

Jesus Christ, not the Adventist church, came down from heaven, died for our sins, and offered His perfect righteousness in our behalf. He alone, therefore, not the church, can save us. He alone is our salvation, not the person who led us to Him, not the pastor, not the

Sabbath School teacher, not the conference evangelist, the academy principal, the church elders, nor the General Conference president. Open their hands. You won't find scars there from the cross. You will find the nail prints only in Christ's hands.

But you say that you've been burned by the church? So was Uriah the Hittite, when the ruler of the remnant church slept with his wife and then had him murdered. You've been hurt by people who should have known better? So was Naboth the Jezreelite, who was killed by the queen who wanted his vineyard for her husband. You've been sickened by injustice, hypocrisy, and the sins of professed Sabbath keepers? So was Isaiah, who wrote a whole book of the Bible about it. You've been treated unjustly by church leadership? So was Jesus, whom remnant-church leaders taunted, jeered, and then hung on a cross.

What else could you expect, considering the history of God's remnant? If the corporate remnant would rebel against Moses, stone the prophets, throw Jeremiah into jail, and hang the Saviour of the world on a cross, what makes you think you're going to be treated any better?

We have an enemy who hates this church, who is seeking to drive people away. Unfortunately, some of his most effective agents have been Seventh-day Adventists themselves, the ones commissioned to bring people in!

Therefore, we have to rise above Seventh-day *Adventists*, who are not the same as Seventh-day *Adventism*. We have to look beyond the messengers to the message itself. We have to see Christ, not those who profess to be Christians. We can't let Seventh-day Adventist members turn us away from Seventh-day Adventist truth.

This truth is not the church. The church might know the truth, but it isn't synonymous with the truth. The truth exists independently of the church, even if this church—more than any other—understands what that truth is. Whatever might happen to the Adventist church, the Adventist truth remains.

The crucial question is: Will we remain with the truth? The answer depends upon our relationship with Him who is the truth Himself. "I am the way, the truth, and the life," Jesus said (John 14:6). Only an enduring experience with Christ and with the truth He has given for this time can lift you above the turmoil and treachery that you will no doubt face in the church if you haven't already.

Be prepared: it's going to take more to stay faithful to God than just knowing about the Sabbath, the state of the dead, and dietary rules. You'll need to know the Lord who has given us those teachings, and not only to know Him, but to love Him. "Thou shalt love the Lord thy God with all thy heart, and with all thy soul, and with all thy mind. This is the first and great commandment" (Matthew 22:37, 38). We are commanded to love God, and therefore we first need to know Him, for how can we love God unless we know Him?

"And this is life eternal, that they might know thee the only true God, and Jesus Christ, whom thou hast sent" (John 17:3). If we know God and love God, then we are going to obey God, despite the pressure that the faithful remnant will face to turn from Him.

And hereby we do know that we know him, if we keep his commandments (1 John 2:3).

He that hath my commandments, and keepeth them, he it is that loveth me (John 14:21).

If a man love me, he will keep my words" (John 14:23).

For this is the love of God, that we keep his commandments" (1 John 5:3).

Here is the patience of the saints: here are they that keep the commandments of God, and the faith of Jesus (Revelation 14:12).

Knowing and loving God is linked to keeping His commandments, and obedience to His commandments is one of the key characteristics of His final remnant. Whoever the people of the remnant are, they will certainly have a personal relationship with God, one that will not back out when faced with severe pressure to disobey. Their love for God will be the fuel that drives them to endure persecution, economic pressure, loss of work, family, maybe even death.

"Have you that strong hold of God, that consecration to His service, that your religion will not fail you in the face of the direst persecution? *The deep love of God alone will sustain the soul amid the trials which are just upon us.*[7]

Thus, we need not only a knowledge of the truth, but more importantly, a continuing experience with Him who is the truth. Jesus wants a relationship with each of us as distinctly as if we were the only person on the earth. In turn, we need a love commitment to Him so strong that we would stay faithful even if the whole Adventist church apostatized, even if everyone turned against us, even if everyone fled— even if we were . . . *the only one left*!

> And it shall come to pass in that day, that the remnant of Israel, and such as are escaped of the house of Jacob, shall no more again depend upon him that smote them: but shall depend upon the Lord, the holy one of Israel, in truth" (Isaiah 10:20).[8]

> Who is a God like unto thee, that pardoneth iniquity, and passeth by the transgression of the remnant of his heritage? he retaineth not his anger for ever, because he delighteth in mercy. He will turn again, he will have compassion upon us; he will subdue our iniquities; and thou wilt cast all their sins into the depths of the sea. Thou wilt perform the truth to Jacob, and the mercy to Abraham, which thou hast sworn unto our fathers from the days of old (Micah 7:18-20).

Here are the saints, here are those who are pardoned and cleansed, whose iniquities are subdued, whose sins are cast into the sea because they depend only upon the Lord, the holy one of Israel, in truth.

Here is the remnant!

---

1. *The Desire of Ages*, 377.
2. Ibid., 383.
3. Ibid., 391.
4. Ibid., 392, 393.
5. *The Great Controversy*, 608.
6. *Testimonies for the Church*, 5:463.
7. Ibid., 135, emphasis supplied.
8. Author's translation.